A BIKER-SOLDIER'S JOURNEY

MONTY VAN HORN

xulon
PRESS

A Biker-Soldier's Journey
by Monty Van Horn

Printed in the United States of America

ISBN 9781628390278

www.xulonpress.com

INTRODUCTION

Do you find yourself wondering why you are going through the storms you are facing, or maybe a storm you have just gone through? Do you feel like you are being singled out? Maybe you think the general population looks at you as a second-class citizen? Are you unable to put your finger on just exactly what is going on in your life or where you are supposed to be going? Do you find yourself questioning if God really has a calling on your life?

In this book, you will learn that you are not alone. Your storms, trials and temptations are shared with millions around you. You may not find the "big answer" by reading this book, but it will encourage you when you realize that the writer is just another ordinary person just like you. You will discover that you are not alone in your search for just what it is that God is calling you to do. With help from God, you may just learn exactly what you are being called to do also!

I wrote this book because my wife has bugged me to write it for 26 years! After God talked to me through her enough times (way too many times) in those 26 years, I figured I either need to write this book or write my obituary. So guess what, you got stuck with this book.

In each chapter, you will get to read of at least one real-life event that took place in my life. You will also come across a comments section for thoughts to ponder. With prayer and an open heart, I believe that each chapter could change your life.

If you don't think God can use an ordinary person like you for his glory, at least read the first chapter and see what he did with me. Oh, and that is just the beginning.

If the Lord ministers to you with any portion of this book, I would love to hear from you at *https://www.facebook.com/ABikerSoldiersJourney*.

CONTENTS

ACKNOWLEDGMENTS

First and foremost, I thank God for leading me in writing this book, as well as giving me the courage and strength to finish it.

About the cover, I want to thank **Photography by Deana C** for not only the photography but the completed design of the cover.

I want to thank the following friends and family for reading the rough draft of this book and providing candid feedback that has made this the book that it has become:

Shannon Adler of Killeen, Texas; I have always enjoyed Shannon's company and was humbled that she offered to proof this book.

Margie Bellomy of Diana, Texas; Margie is my sister-in-law, but so much more than that. Margie has been a friend and is a sister in Christ.

Deana Connell of Belton, Texas; I have known Deana the least amount of time than all who is listed here, but she has become a close friend and Ethan's "God Mother."

Dale Estes of Diana, Texas; My father-in-law, like his daughter, has been more than an in-law. He is a friend and has been an inspiration.

Pete Harvey of Longview, Texas; My brother-in-law who also loves to ride. I prayed for him to get saved for twelve years and God finally brought him into his fold! Hallelujah!

Beth Schimschock of Copperas Cove, Texas; She is a friend and one of my parishioners. I fell in love with her and her friend their first visit to our church. I preached the unadulterated truth of God, and she was mad at me for quite some time. That is probably why we love each other now.

Mark Simms of Florence, Texas; God has used Mark in many ways and some of which you will get to read about. Mark is a true friend, mentor, boss, but most of all my brother in Christ.

And a special thank you to my wife, lover and best friend, **Tammy Van Horn**, for your continued support and encouragement that motivated me to write this book. Thanks Babe, I love you twice as much!

DEDICATION

This book is dedicated to all the fallen heroes that gave the ultimate sacrifice that helped make this country what it is today. A few that I personally knew are mentioned in this book. To one soldier that I want to give a distinguished honor to is:

SSG (RET) Walter A. Taflinger (1941–2012)

This excerpt from his orders for an Army Commendation Medal with V device says more than I can:

For heroism, in connection with military operations against a hostile force in the Republic of Vietnam, Sergeant Walter A. Taflinger distinguished himself by exceptionally valorous actions on 24 February 1969 while assigned to the 1099th transportation company. While serving as Chief Engineer on a landing craft, which was participating in operations on the Buong River south of Long Binh, the craft came under intense hostile small arms, rocket and automatic weapons fire. With total disregard for his own safety, Sergeant Taflinger rushed from the engine room to a stern window and began placing effective fire upon the enemy positions. Sergeant Taflinger was wounded several times during the ensuing battle, but refused medical evacuation until he had thoroughly checked the craft for damage. His alert and aggressive actions contributed significantly to the defeat of the enemy force, and earned him the respect and admiration of all with whom he served. His bravery and devotion to duty under extremely hazardous conditions was in keeping with the highest traditions of the military service, and reflects great credit upon himself, his unit and the United States Army.

> The memory of SSG Walter A. Taflinger lives on forever. He was a friend, mentor, my hero and my uncle.

AN ANSWER FROM GOD

Monty was sitting on the back steps, talking to God about a predicament he had just found himself in! He had just received his seventh and final grade from the intense Bible Study that he had been taking for the last year! It was another A+, which is not hard to get since it is an open book test. All he had to do was open up the King James Version of the Bible and look up the answers. Each test had 300 questions. The dilemma was not that he had received another A+, but that there was a slip of paper he could fill out and send in with $25, and he could be an ordained minister!

He took a long drag off his Marlboro and a huge gulp of his Old Milwaukee. Monty had just come from inside the house, where he had shared with Tammy about the slip of paper and commented sarcastically about what a joke it was! This was after she had asked him if he was going to send the "application" in. After his snide comment, he added, "Besides, I didn't know this was an ordination course! I thought it was a Bible Study course!"

Tammy smacked the spatula into the skillet on the stove. "Really, Honey?" She shifted her hips in that defiant motion all married men have seen before. She placed her free hand on her hip to accent her intent of mockery and pointed her spatula at Monty. He looked at her, anticipating his next response, and noticed the fresh grease dripping from the spatula landing onto the kitchen linoleum. His eyes met hers and he knew there was no reason to say anything. Then her words seared his every thought; "You recon' God didn't know it was an ordination course?"

His face became flushed in a deep red as he became angry! He didn't say a word, just headed to the back door of their two bedroom trailer house and took a seat on the back steps. You could find him there every day after work; looking out over their 35 acres, drinking a beer and smoking a cigarette. Monty didn't smoke in the house, so you could find him on the back steps daily. He wasn't usually talking out loud to God, but he didn't know what else to do. He set his fleece out before the Lord that day *(Judges 6:36-40)*.

It was simple; he was sure that God didn't want him to be a preacher, as they had already been down this road together more than once. In fact, the reason he left the military in 1992 was to become an ordained minister and return to the military as a chaplain. That was seven years ago. God had made it clear that he wasn't supposed to be a preacher. So once Monty had convinced himself that he knew this was a joke, he simply said, "God, if you want me to send that slip in and be an ordained minister," he made sarcastic motions with his hands, "then, Lord, you take this," he lifted up his Milwaukee as if to make sure God knew what he was talking about, "and this," he waved his cigarette in the air.

Monty went on to explain to the Lord *[how many of us have tried to explain to God what we are "really" saying–LOL]* that he knew that if he was to be an ordained man of God that he couldn't be doing those things. He was convinced that he had to live by a different set of standards as a man of God (I Timothy 3:1-13).

Monty said, "Just take it away from me, Lord. You do that, and I will never turn back or question you! I will send the paperwork in."

A few minutes later, a very frustrated wife opened the back door; "supper is ready." Her voice was that of submission and, at the same time, sadness. Monty got up and went inside with his wife. Their prayer was a very short one, and they ate their supper in silence.

The very next day, after a long 12 hours at work, Monty drove the 45-minute drive to their homestead. He walked in the door and Tammy was cooking supper, as usual. He walked to the refrigerator and opened the door. His shelf that was designated for his beer was about half full. He subconsciously reached for an Old Milwaukee, but stopped suddenly. He didn't want one! He was still bent over staring at a shelf half full of nothing but his beer. "Oh My God!" he exclaimed. Tammy shuddered, "Honey, what's wrong? I know there is beer in there; I already checked." Tammy was the obedient wife and always took care of Monty. Yes, she made sure his beer was cold and that he didn't run out of cigarettes. Cigarettes! He touched his shirt pocket for the first time that day. He uttered loudly, "OH MY GOD!" Tammy was concerned, "What Honey, what?" He stood up, turned around to face her. Tammy had never really seen that kind of look on his face. He was staring at her, still clutching his chest! Was it a heart attack? "Honey!" she spoke loudly.

He looked at her. As his eyes focused on hers, he saw the look of shock and bewilderment on her face. She was obviously concerned as she stared at him. Then he started telling her about yesterday. As he told her about his conversation with God and him putting his fleece out, she became more and more excited. When he finished by telling her he didn't want a beer and that he hadn't smoked a cigarette all day and doesn't want one, she gave a Holy Ghost laugh. "You are going to send the application in then, right?" He looked at her, still numb from his own testimony, "Of course! I don't have a choice!" Tammy did the Pentecostal Hallelujah Dance in the kitchen with her spatula held high. Monty watched her dancing around and around, but was numb to emotion. He wasn't excited, anxious, afraid, happy or cheerful; he was nothing. He was just numb.

> *[Have you ever prayed to God and not expected an answer? Have you ever laid your fleece out, knowing that there would not be a response? Down deep you knew that was just "Old Testament Religion." We all have to some degree, amen? Have you ever heard the saying, "Be careful what you ask for because you just might get it?" (1 John 5:14-15) I would like to ask you to meditate on these "thoughts to ponder" or "Just saying..." sections and ask God to reveal what*

13

*he wants you to see. Maybe, just maybe, God is
waiting for you to put the fleece out. Amen?]*

Tammy turned back to her task of getting supper ready, and Monty walked outside. He looked over the land as he did every day, but this time without a lit cigarette or a cold beer. The Lord had delivered him from alcohol and tobacco, which he had been in bondage to for nearly a quarter of a century. He started walking around, looking at the property through blurry eyes as the tears started swelling up. He was changed! That was Friday the 15th of December 2000, the beginning of his new life. Monty was back on the path that God had set forth from the beginning of time.

He was now on that path that God had started him on in 1973 on February 11th. That was a night that friends of the family had taken him and his sister, Marty, to an evening church service. He doesn't remember anything about that service except at the end. To this day, he remembers looking through the same blurry eyes at the speaker up front. He could not move fast enough to get to the front on his knees and ask Jesus into his life! Now, 27 years later, he felt the same fresh anointing on his life! Not at an altar call. Not at a revival. No, this was personal and it was intimate. God made it loud and clear to him. God wanted him to be his servant.

Tammy sent the "application" off, with the $25 fee enclosed, the very next day. She didn't want to give satan a chance to get his slimy foot back in the door with her husband. She was living through an answered prayer, and she was excited. She had actually had a vision and had shared it with Monty back in 1986 that he was going to be a preacher. When he had decided to leave the army in 1991 to become an ordained minister, she thought she was seeing the fulfillment of the vision then. She was ecstatic and, at the same time, scared that now after all these years it was going to finally happen!

As she drove "Big Ben," their 1997 F350 crew cab, to Gatesville with the envelope that was changing their future, she thought about back in 1986 when she had told her husband that he was going to be a preacher. She smiled to herself, the look on his face was priceless when she had told him that, and now it was coming true! She shook her head as she thought, "I better not say I told you so!"

[I called this ordination a "cracker box preacher" prize. Even after I first received it in the mail, I was underestimating God's ordination! Not the best way to start, is it? But, I was honestly still in shock of what God was doing in my life! Besides, you have to go to seminary to be a REAL PREACHER! Right? You will see in my second book (if there is one) that my "spiritual mentors" didn't consider this ordination a "real one" either. I want to encourage the reader right now! If God has called you and ordained you to be something for him (no matter what it is), you are authorized by God himself! What school or piece of paper can stand up to that? Just saying....]

A CLUELESS ORDAINED MINISTER JOINS CMA

Less than two months later Monty, now an "ordained minister" and clueless to what he was to do next, was in the backyard soaking up the Texas sun. It was a beautiful Saturday morning in February, and yet felt like it was summer. He thought about the 1984 Honda Goldwing Aspencade that had been sitting in the small portable storage building for the short Texas winter. He decided to give it a bath and take pictures so he could advertise it in the local paper. After a couple hours, it looked immaculate. Monty stepped back, admiring his work. He was sweating from his workout and was ready to take her on a road test.

After explaining to Tammy that he better take it for a short ride and make sure everything is in top shape before soliciting prospective buyers, he pulled out of their quarter-mile drive in Levita and hit the back roads. As he headed towards Ater and then Jonesboro, he thought back to when he met Tammy, and all he owned was a motorcycle. Riding was in his blood, and he loved being in the wind. The weather wasn't really an issue for him; he just loved the freedom of being in the saddle. In fact, it was a dark and very cold winter night that he rode nearly 200 miles to meet Tammy on that CB750 Custom.

Two Broken Hearts Meet

Monty met Tammy on 31 December 1985. Ironically, it was Monty and his current wife's anniversary. But, his current wife was now in love with another man. That man was Tammy's husband! Tammy had done some research and found Monty, because she wanted to see if he would like to have love letters her husband had that were written by his wife. His adrenaline was pumped up as he mounted his iron horse and headed to Diana, Texas. It was going to be about a 200-mile ride. He was going into unfamiliar territory, and it was going to take about 4 hours to get there. The last instruction was to call from the Nobles Grocery store in Diana, Texas as soon as he got there.

Monty arrived in record time and, to this date, is still the record for him! He made the call, and the folks were nervous as they told him to hide beside the store. Within a few minutes a vehicle pulled up, shining its lights on him. Monty leaned forward from his semi-relaxed posture on the bike and threw his cigarette down. He dismounted the bike to go see if this was who he was waiting on when the woman in the passenger side snapped, "Follow us quickly!" Monty slipped his helmet on, as the vehicle backed up, and faced US Highway 259.

When he started his bike, the truck took off like it was a race! The couple in the truck was not messing around! Monty didn't really mind traveling down a US highway or interstate at high speeds. But when this couple turned onto a country road and he was doing 90 MPH, he was praying he didn't hit a deer!

A few minutes later, the truck pulled into the drive of a small home. Monty pulled in and parked in the front yard next to them. Before he could even shut off the bike, a lady came running and waving her arms, "No, not there." Monty looked at the fanatical woman approaching him, "Behind the house, you have to hide the bike behind the house!" Her face was inches from his, and she was a knockout! He thought to himself, "If this is Tammy, what kind of idiot would run off with my wife if he had this?" Monty nodded and pulled his bike around back, wondering what in the world he has gotten himself into! Hide! Hide! Hide! What is wrong with all these people?

He had an older man guiding him to where he wanted Monty to put the bike, and two children with boards following him. "Right there, son," The older man said. Monty shut her off and the children handed their grandpa the boards for the kickstand. After getting his girl sitting on her kickstand in a stable manner, the family escorted him inside the house. There was the knockout, smiling from ear to ear; "You must be cold! Do you want some coffee? Take your clothes off." Monty smiled as he nodded his head for the coffee and started taking his gloves off so he could remove his helmet. He thought to himself, "Take my clothes off, huh?" Then she said, "I am Margie, this is my husband, Bennie." Monty nodded and shook Bennie's hand. He put his emotions into check, "Ok, it figures she was married. So where is the overweight slob that is married to my wife's lover?" he thought to himself.

Then Monty was introduced to Dale and LaRece Estes, Margie's parents, and all the children running around in the house. Then Margie smiled bigger as she set the coffee on the table in front of Monty, "Tammy, my sister, is on her way over here." Monty nodded in thanks, and then asked, "Why am I hiding my bike?" Monty learned that his wife and Tammy's husband were living only 10 minutes away and travel the same road all the time.

Then Dale piped up, "You burned up the highway, son! You beat your wife here!" Monty looked bewildered. Margie noticed his confusion, "Your wife is going to drive right past the Nobles Grocery, and it's on the way to their place!" Monty didn't have a clue where his wife had moved the trailer house! He had taken out a loan for their mobile home to be moved and gave her the money. She was adamant that she needed her space. Now he understood why. Margie and Bennie talked Monty into going with them to a New Year's Party while they waited for Tammy to show up. He was finally warming up and decided to start removing his outer clothing. Just as he started to stand up, a car pulled into the drive, "My sister is here." Margie replied, while looking out the kitchen window.

Monty was standing up when the door opened, and his mouth almost dropped open when Tammy walked in! But, he kept his poker face on the best he could while inside he jumped with a WOW! He nodded and shook Tammy's hand, thinking, "Oh man! Whoever ran off with my wife is for sure a complete idiot!" Within a few minutes Tammy and Monty were sitting at the kitchen table, reading letters that his wife had sent to her husband! That night, they held each other with tears of pain. They shared with each other their heartaches. They fell in love...

[Has your life ever fallen apart? Has a secured relationship that you thought could never get any better suddenly change and just dissipate into thin air while reading a "Dear John" letter? Then later, when all the dust from the storm settles, you see that God has something really special in store for you (Jeremiah 29:11). Sometimes it happens faster than others, but it always takes longer than we want. Let God do it in his time. Amen? He said, "I will never leave you or forsake you," (Hebrews 13:5). But he didn't promise that we would not have to endure some storms! There was a storm before Peter walked on water, amen? I know you have heard the first part of a saying many times; "When God closes one door, he always opens another." Don't you hate hearing that when you're in the hallway? I did too, until one time I was going through a really tough time and a young but mature Christian told me, "You know what they say, 'when God closes one door he always opens another!'" I wanted to scream, but then she grabbed my arm and said, "What no one ever tells you is that the hallway is a living hell while you are waiting on the other door to open."]

* * *

Monty downshifted his 1984 Goldwing at the little community park in Turnersville. He realized he had been riding a whole lot longer than he had insinuated to Tammy. He pulled his cell phone out and confirmed that he had been riding the back roads of Coryell County for right at an hour. He thought about heading straight home, but he was still a half an hour away. He dialed the home number, knowing he was going to get a very displeased woman on the other end. The phone rang only once, "You are going to keep the bike, aren't you?" snapped Tammy. Monty nodded, "Yeah, I think so, Babe." he meekly replied. He informed her where he was and about how long it would be before he got back home.

Monty arrived home to a woman with something to say. She was standing at the east end of their two-bedroom trailer house when he pulled up on the bike. Her arms crossed and folded, and her right foot tapping the ground hard! He tried to smile as he rode right past her, and she cocked her head in that "You have had it" attitude. He just knew he was going to get an earful when he got off the bike. He pulled his iron horse into the portable building that was the designated stall for her. As he walked out, she made a simple statement; "If we are going to ride, we need to do it for God!" Monty looked at her as she walked back towards the house. Wow! That wasn't bad, he thought. He smiled in agreement to himself.

* * *

April of 2001: Monty and Tammy were card carrying CMA'ers! They were members of the Warriors of the Way chapter of the Christian Motorcyclists Association in Killeen, Texas. They were riding for the Son. Things were moving fast. One of the things that the CMA'ers do is to preach the Gospel on the highways and byways at different secular rallies. It seemed like God had Monty right where he wanted him.

It had only been four months since the transformation of God on Monty's life, and new friends were coming into their life every day. These new friends laughed at jokes that weren't funny before the transformation.

> *[You know those clean jokes that you never really told anyone because they were "corny." Many of the old friends were staying in touch, but not sticking around or coming over as often to visit.]*

Monty and Mark McDowell (Mack) used to get together almost every weekend and shoot up clay pigeons while putting away a case or more of beer. Monty just wasn't the beer-drinking, Marlboro-smoking, party animal he used to be. Mack and Monty had been close, and spent many weekends at the farm. The living room couch was Mack's weekend bed. It wasn't long, and Mack wasn't going out to the farm anymore. They just didn't have the same interests anymore. It just happens! *[Ephesians 4:22-24]*

> *[Have you given your life to Jesus, but still have the same friends and doing the same things you did before you gave your life to HIM? If so, you need to evaluate the validity of your walk with Jesus (1 Corinthians 15:33). I am not saying you need to go shun your old friends! NO! There is a "religious" teaching that when we put on the new, we need to remove the old out of our lives! The truth is that when we put on the new, the old will leave on its own, amen? Listen carefully; if you have truly changed, your old friends will be "uncomfortable" and will spend less time around you. Mack and I are still friends and always will be, but we don't hang out together, amen? That is life; it just happens.]*

It really seemed like Monty and Tammy were on the right path for the first time in their almost 15 years of marriage. Everyone was so friendly in this new world that they now belonged to. Well, almost.....

REJECTED BY YOUR "OWN KIND"

In April of 2001, on a Sunday after church, Monty and Tammy were riding their Goldwing in Evant, Texas when suddenly the bike shut off. Monty quickly checked the traffic and coasted into a church parking lot. Tammy helped push the big bagger to a nice shade tree just a few feet away. Monty called his pastor at Twin Creeks Christian Center in Gatesville. "Hello?" answered his pastor. Monty sighed, "Pastor Steve, we need a favor." Pastor Steve promised to get the message to Matthew, their youngest son, to come help them. Pastor Steve also went on to say that the pastor of the church that they were at was a friend of his and that if they needed anything, just ask.

While waiting on the phone call from their youngest son, Monty removed the seat and side panels. He started using the multi-meter he had stowed in the saddlebag to fault isolate the problem. While working on the bike, he and Tammy finished off the water they had with them; the Texas heat was brutal! Monty had determined that the battery was completely dead. They heard a vehicle, and watched as it sped past them only to abruptly slow down and stop in a parking space at the church. The folks got out and went inside. Tammy sighed, "I wonder what that was all about?" Monty shrugged, "I don't have a clue, Babe. I guess they are in a hurry to be the first ones to the church." Another vehicle came by, slowed down, rolled down their windows and started laughing as they drove on to another vacant parking spot!

Monty had sweat dripping off his brow as he stood up and looked at the young adults getting out of the vehicle, still laughing and having a good time. Monty watched them go inside. He looked over at his wife, who was a mess. Tammy asked, "What's wrong?" He chuckled, "You recon' this church don't like bikers?"

The cell phone rang, and it was his son, Matthew. Monty told Matt where another motorcycle battery was that had a good charge and asked him to bring them the battery and some water.

Monty and Tammy moved along with the shade from the tree that they were under. The bike, on the other hand, sat where it was, dead. The thoughts that were running through Monty and Tammy's mind were not of Christ. They were sulking over the way folks had come into the church parking lot, and not a single vehicle stopped to offer assistance. The salt in the wound was the fact that it was "Christians" now currently inside their church, singing praises to their God. Monty shook his head at the last derogatory comment that Tammy made and said, "Honey, God is trying to show us something." She sighed, "Well Honey, what do you think God is trying to tell them?" He laughed quietly, "It doesn't matter, Babe; they aren't listening."

[Have you ever been so busy making a loud noise to the Lord that you can't hear what he is trying to tell you? (1 Kings 19:12) Have you or do you know someone so busy for the Lord that they don't have time for the world? You know that religious spirit I am talking about! Some of us have been caught up in it too. We find ourselves running a "100 miles an hour" to do for God and fly right by an injured warrior, being too busy to notice or care. Maybe because they were not dressed as we expected or riding what we expected? Maybe they were doing something we disapprove of so we refused to stop and help them? Praise the Lord for his Son, Jesus Christ, who stopped for the Tax collector and prostitute! Lord, help all of us be more like Jesus every day! Amen? The Lord was showing us something very specific to our newfound ministry that HE had us in.]

23

It seemed like forever while the couple waited for their son to arrive. Monty was listening to the church music and the voices lifting praises to their God, while calculating the time frame his son should arrive. There was a good chance that church would be over before Matt arrived. He was correct. Tammy and Monty had sat there, sweating profusely while listening to the Hymns being sung, and then a long silence, which was obviously the message being given.

Tammy piped up again, "Honey, what do you think the message is about?" Monty shook his head as he replied sarcastically, "The Love of God and going out and letting their lights shine for God's Glory." Tammy giggled. Monty was quietly asking God what it was that he was supposed to learn from this.

The doors of the church opened, and the Sunday evening crowd rushed to their vehicles. To be shunned as a second-class citizen while going to the church was one thing but when every vehicle left the same way they came, Monty and Tammy were speechless. They literally looked at each other when the last vehicle drove past them and onto their next destination. The vehicles were driving within a couple feet of them. The people would not look at them, minus the same vehicle that rolled down their windows to laugh on the way into the parking lot. They made sure to roll their window down and laugh on the way out as well!

Tammy was ranting about all these brothers and sisters in Christ that didn't even offer to stop and give them a bottle of water. Monty shook his head and Tammy stopped, "What! You can't tell me this isn't bothering you." Monty nodded in agreement, "But I'm not mad, Babe. God is showing us how the people that we are trying to reach are looked at by the people that we are." She looked confused, "The people that we are?" He nodded, "Christians." Tammy thought for a moment and sighed, "Wow. That is what God wants us to see?" He nodded in silence while still waiting for their son, and trying to create some saliva for his now very dry mouth. Monty's thoughts focused on the "preacher" that didn't stop either. He thought about the Samaritan that stopped to help when the spiritual leaders didn't *[Luke 10:30-35]*.

24

[We, Christians, have to be careful to stifle the Pharisees and Sadducees spirit in us! Churches have a set of "unspoken standards" that isn't published anywhere but in the minds of the pastor and congregation. Sometimes, that standard is what we wear, especially to church. Other times it is what type of vehicle we drive. But Jesus showed us by example that none of that really matters to him. He wants your heart. Amen?]

Tammy broke the silence, "I just don't get it. Our patch says we are Christians." Monty remembered a similar situation when he was in high school, and shared it with his wife; "Did I ever tell you the time...?

Our Sunday Best

"Marty, you ready?" asked Monty. His sister answered, "Yes, almost." He shook his head. Doesn't she realize that the correct answer would have been no? He headed for the 1969 Ford LTD; "I'm heading to the car." By the time he had the car running good enough that he didn't have to flutter the accelerator to keep her running, Marty jumped into the passenger side of the car. The family had moved to Lewisville, and the two teenagers wanted to find a church. There was a church just a few miles up the road and, due to not having any money for fuel, it was the best deal for their first church visit. Both of them were actually excited to be going to church and had saved their best church clothes for the occasion!

[Note to reader! When your children are excited about going to church, TAKE THEM! DON'T SEND them, TAKE THEM!! Just saying......]

While sitting in the back of this small and quaint church, Monty noticed that quite a few folks would turn and look at them. Monty also noticed that there was not one single person their age in the church. In fact, they must have found the church where all the oldest of the community met. It seemed like everyone was old enough to be their grandpas and grandmas. The old hymns were great, and the message was a standard one. Even if there were no other teenagers, they could at least attend there until later.

This older gentleman met them at the door with a million dollar smile, and Monty just knew they had found a home church. It was so close to the house, too. The tall man bent at his waist, while still smiling, and shook Monty's hand. Monty gave the man back a gentleman's squeeze as the man stopped shaking his hand, but continued to keep a firm grip, and said, "We really enjoyed having you two here today. But, we wear our Sunday best at this church." Monty's face turned red as he looked at his sister and saw that she was on fire as well.

> *[Nope, we never went back to that church. We didn't go to any church for a while. Have you ever visited a dying church? It is easy to identify a dying church. They are getting more and more popular in our country. It is one with a half empty parking lot and has old people inside that have those set standards I talked about earlier. It is the churches that preach that they want to reach out to the un-churched, but in reality they don't want the un-churched in their church! They sit in their pews preaching people into hell, instead of pulling them out of satan's snare (Matthew 25:40)].*

* * *

Tammy was in awe, "I don't remember you ever telling me that story!" Monty laughed, "Just thought of it. It is kind of like how we just got treated this evening." Matthew was pulling up! Praise the Lord. The first thing the couple did was drink an entire bottle of water and then started sipping on a second one. They shared with their son what they had just experienced. He was surprised and said that Pastor Steve had told him this was a good church.

It only took a few minutes, and the bike was up and running. Monty checked it and it was charging, too. He thanked the Lord loudly for having only a dead battery and a good charging system. An hour later, the family was back at Van

Horn Acres, soaking up some cool air and drinking some more ice-cold water.

> *[I know that this is a common thing, and many of the readers can relate to similar situations in their lives. I just ask you to calm down and ask God what he is **showing you**. If you still haven't got a clue, and it has been years or if it has only been hours, **ask God to reveal** to you what he wants you to see (Amos 3:7). I hope this story helps in that revelation from God! Now, both these instances are from churches that didn't know me from Adam. But, what if you receive the same type of offense from a church that is supposed to know you and love you? You know, like family?]*

It was in the fall of 2001, and Monty and Tammy had just come in from a weekend-long rally. It was a chilly day, and the chaps and leather jackets were a welcome garment for sure. It was Sunday afternoon and they stopped in at the Gatesville HEB to get a few things before heading out to the farm to "lick their wounds." The couple was very tired, but so thankful for God's grace and mercy HE brought to those that gave their lives over to him this past weekend. That made it all worth it. The weekend campout and letting their lights shine for the Lord had an impact, and God now had some new sheep in his fold!

As they got into the isle, they noticed two children looking at them and smiling. Monty got Tammy's attention and motioned to her in silence. They were standing behind a Pastor's wife that they knew, and the kids always liked them. The Pastor's wife noticed that both her young children were staring and smiling back at the people behind her. As she turned slightly sideways to see what the children were looking at, Monty was prepared to give her a big smile and hug. But when she looked down at the child, she looked sideways at Monty's leather chaps and quickly turned the two children around and made them face the front of the store! Monty looked back at Tammy, who was in total shock!

Monty was about to tap her on the shoulder, but was stopped. Not by Tammy, but by God. God was showing him something! The Pastor's wife never turned the slightest and made sure her children stayed facing forward from then on. She paid for her merchandise and briskly walked out the door!

[To this day, that is the longest five minutes we have ever experienced in line at a grocery store! The next time we were at church (yes it was our own Pastor's wife), the children that used to smile and think we were the neat people on bikes came right up to me and kicked me in the shin! Wow! To this day, the pastor's wife doesn't know we were the ones behind her (unless she reads this book). We had reached a point in our walk that we didn't take offense easy. It is satan that wants you to take offense (Matthew 24:10). We realized that God wants us to learn from these different experiences, and HE was allowing them to happen to open our eyes. It is incidents like this one that has helped mold me into the biker preacher that I am today. How can you take offense at that?

Praise you, Lord, for opening my eyes. He is trying to tell you the same thing about a similar situation in your life. Has a fellow Christian "shunned" you because of your clothing? Was it a Christian in a leadership position? You are not alone. Actually, you are in good company with tax collectors and a lonely widow woman with only two mites (Mark 12:42-44). Just hang in there. Whatever you do, don't take offense! God allowed all of these incidents to happen to mold me! Thus, I thank God for each one of those situations, amen? You need to as well.]

A LESSON ON INTEGRITY

In the summer of 2001, Tammy and Monty had their 1984 Aspencade loaded to the gills, as well as a trailer they were towing. Monty had done a test ride without Tammy and, after a couple changes in weight distribution, was satisfied that he was ready. The only thing was that they still didn't have a legal tag on the trailer. Monty was anxious to get on the road and didn't care about such insignificant issues. Monty put the dilly boat trailer tag on the little camper. Tammy reminded him that they were currently going through classes on integrity at church. Her comments fell on deaf ears as he finished tying the final things down for the night. "We are leaving at daylight, Babe, period." She sighed, "Ok." He added, "Besides the only way anyone would ever know is if we were in an accident or something."

The next day, after a 250-mile ride, the couple was at Margie and Benny's for a two-night stay. It was amazing how many people would "rubberneck" when they went by pulling this trailer behind their bike. After a couple nights, it was time to head to Indiana. After a series of goodbyes and a prayer from the family, they were on their way.

The number one concern was that it was still a little foggy and lots of dew on the ground. They had only been on the road a few short miles when Tammy started moving around excessively. Monty was concerned and turned halfway around to ask what was wrong. She replied that she was adjusting herself. Monty turned back around to see that he had just steered the bike off into the grassy embankment of a deep bar ditch! As he tried to lean left to bring the bike back to the road, the rear tire started slipping! Monty had no choice but to steer into the slide and give it some throttle, bringing the bike back upright and down into the bar ditch!

At the bottom of the three-foot deep ditch, the trailer gave the bike a push up the opposite embankment and sent the rear tire into a slide to the left! Again, steering into the slide and throttle brought the bike back upright in time to head back down the embankment! This procedure repeated itself many times with the height getting less and less until Monty had control of the bike, heading straight down at the bottom of the bar ditch at 50MPH! All he had to do now was stop, but up ahead just a few more feet was a huge concrete culvert! It would be impossible to stop in time!

Monty gave her full throttle and tried to climb out of the ditch! The bike was willing, and made it over halfway up before the trailer started taking them into a slide again! Laying the bike down and relaxing was the last thing! They both tumbled in the air like rag dolls for 122 feet before coming to rest in the bar ditch.

[Any basic motorcycle rider course instructor will tell you that where a biker looks, he will go! In other words, do NOT look off to the side of the road or you will end up on the side of the road! Many one-bike accidents in the curves is because the rider looks somewhere besides where he wants to go! Our walk with Jesus is the same way! When we look somewhere besides at Jesus, we will find ourselves in a series of slides in the bar ditch of trials and tribulations, and straight for the culvert of hell! Jesus told us to keep our eyes on the plow, amen? (Read Luke 9:62)]

Tammy was moaning, and Monty could feel the shaft of something impaled through his abdomen! His eyes were closed and he didn't want to see what it was, but he was sure it was a T-post or something similar! He slid his hands towards the exit wound so he could feel how big around it was. He thought to himself, "I am going to die impaled on a piece of scrap rebar in a ditch in East Texas!" Tammy moaned again.

He felt nothing! He searched his abdomen where the pain was coming from, but there was nothing sticking out. Then he did what everyone is taught not to do, and took his helmet off. He saw a man standing by the upside down trailer, still attached to the bike. "You want me to call an ambulance?" Monty nodded quickly as he looked at his wife, "Yes, please!" As Monty started moving towards Tammy, the stranger cautioned him to lie still. Monty got next to his wife, laid hands on her and started praying! The man called 911 and assured them that help was on the way.

In the emergency room, Monty was waiting for the results on the x-rays when the police officer entered the room. The man was very polite as he asked about the injuries and where they had been headed. Monty shared with him about what their plans had been. Then the deputy asked, "Sir, do you own a dilly boat trailer?" Monty started laughing. The deputy cocked his head to the side a little, resembling a dog that wants to understand what you are trying to say. Monty laughed a little harder, grabbing his gut as the pain seared through him. The deputy asked, "I'm not sure what is so funny about the question." Monty sighed, "You see, my wife and I are taking a class on integrity at our church back home. You, sir, are here to give me the final lesson." The deputy was still oblivious as to what he was talking about, but Monty shared with him that he didn't want to wait to get the legal plates and his wife had reminded him about the class. Then his final comment was that no one would ever know unless, and the deputy finished the sentence, "you were in an accident."

The deputy laughed, "Sir, I have some people in my unit that ride and they need to know your people." Monty must have looked bewildered as the deputy added, "They need to know Jesus." Monty smiled as he reached into his vest pocket and pulled out a clump of business cards, along with some sod and grass. The officer took the whole mess and gave Monty the ticket.

[There are so many thoughts to ponder here. God used an accident to bring a deputy into contact with a Christian, and actually request information on the Christian group because he

31

has lost souls that work with him! Amen? Oh, and God will finish any course you are taking with a situation if you don't adhere to what you are learning yourself (Proverbs 28:9)! Therefore, we need to APPLY what we learn in Bible studies to our lives! I wonder if I would have ever had the accident if I had stayed home and got the correct tag for the trailer Hmmmm, who knows, right? Our Lord does.]

INJURED WARRIORS HELP
INJURED WARRIORS

Marty, Monty's sister, picked up Tammy and Monty at the Longview hospital. They stayed at Pete and Marty's that night, and the next morning were in unbelievable pain. A phone call was made to their youngest, and he drove to East Texas to pick them up. The painkillers were keeping them both numb, but it was obvious that they needed further medical attention. They wanted to get home as soon as possible to see their doctor. Monty spent 45 days off work while going through physical therapy. During that time of being homebound, minus trips to the physical therapist, there was not a single visitor from the church. The pastor never made a house call or even a telephone call. He had seen them the same day they returned in town and knew about the accident. What was God trying to tell them this time?

Monty and Tammy did have a repeating visitor. Chuck Adams came by almost every day. The first visit he had a hot, home-cooked meal with him. He wasn't from the church family. He was the man that they had shown the love of Christ. Chuck had made one visit to their church. He was the one that smelled like a brewery when he entered the church. Yes, he was in bondage to alcohol. His reception wasn't what Tammy and Monty had hoped for. Needless to say, Chuck never made another visit. But guess who showed up with a hot supper for Monty and Tammy? Not just the first night home, but for the next few days until they were able to get around better. Every time he showed up, he reeked of alcohol. Chuck showed the injured couple the true love that Christ wants us to show for one another.

> *[Yes, Chuck was an injured warrior on the battlefield of life! He had lost so many things to alcohol and would return to it as a dog to its vomit (Proverbs 26:11)! His own family was a total case of instability over his drunkenness. Yet, this broken soldier brought two physically-wounded warriors a hot meal when they needed it! Did I say something about the Samaritan versus the religious ones before? We need to show the love of Christ (1 John 4:9-12). Yes, at first we took offense at our Christian family, but God was breaking down the clay and remolding us. He was teaching us about the field of harvest he knew he would be placing us in and in his time. We have lost contact with Chuck, but pray that God has delivered him from the demon of alcoholism and he has a new life.]*

TOO BLESSED TO BE STRESSED – REALLY?

Monty had been doing really well in physical therapy, and it had only been about 14 days or so! He had already learned from his therapist that 30 days would likely be the minimum time off from work, due to the seriousness of his back injury. But, being Monty, he was determined to be back on his feet and at work in less than 30 days. Yvonne, his therapist, was careful with her words and made sure to not get his hopes up too much, but he could tell that she was impressed with his progress.

Then, on a Monday morning, he woke up with extreme pain and very limited movement. Tammy had to help him out of the bed, and then she had to help him to the truck. Tammy drove him to Gatesville for his therapy session. Tammy was so sad, and Monty was perplexed. They talked about how bad he felt and was unable to do things that he had been able to do. The session was agonizing, to say the least! During the last few minutes of the session, Yvonne asked him if there was anything wrong at work. Monty chuckled, "I can't go back to work until I get a release from you." She nodded, "That's right. Then is there anything wrong at home?" Monty was shocked at her intrusive question. He was still trying to figure out exactly how to answer the question. Was she asking about how he and his wife were getting along?

She must have noticed his confusion, "Monty, we have taken about a two-week step backwards. Our progress didn't just stop. We have regressed to almost day one!" Monty shook his head in disbelief; just last Friday he was certain he

35

would be back to work in a couple of weeks! "Monty," Yvonne interrupted his thoughts, "is there anything going on that is causing any stress?" While he looked at her, she added, "I mean anything that wasn't going on the first two weeks of our therapy?" Monty nodded and explained that a couple of his boys had come back home to stay, and their lifestyle wasn't what him or Tammy approved of. He went on to explain how the weekend had been a blur of stressful events with his boys. She shook her head when he was done. "Stress is a killer, sir. You really do not need to be dealing with any stress right now. Actually, we should try to eliminate stress from our lives, period. It is a true killer."

Monty walked lamely back to the truck in more pain than before the therapy. He was exhausted and just wanted to lie down. Tammy got out and opened the door. He entered the F150 four-wheel drive truck like an 80-year-old man. As Tammy drove home, she asked, "Did she say what is wrong?" Monty sighed, "Yes, she did. She said it was stress."

When they arrived home, Monty went straight to bed. Hours later, Monty woke up to silence. He listened hard and could hear nothing! He slowly slid out of the bed and shuffled into the front room to find his wife reading. She looked up, startled; "You ok, Honey? Do you need help? Why didn't you call me?" Monty shrugged off the barrage of questions, "I'm fine. Where are the boys?" She looked back at her book, "They are gone!" Tammy got up and got Monty a glass of tea to drink, while he sat down in his chair. She added, "They won't be coming back either." As she handed him the glass, she said, "No more stress, Honey."

[It is very common for me to tell people I am too blessed to be stressed! Amen? But there are times in our lives that God leaves the job of removing the stress in our lives strictly up to us! It is a choice you have to make! Our life is full of choices, and we refuse to make the right one and continue to live in a stressful situation. I personally didn't believe the "myth" that stress causes physical issues. This event in my life made me re-evaluate my belief on that. My wife knew from experience

*what stress can do to you. While I was asleep,
she told the boys to leave and find some other
place to live! We had a choice to make, and she
made it! Bottom line, we have to have a sound
heart and peace of mind to have a healthy body
(Proverbs 14:30)]*

After a total of 45 days of physical therapy, Monty was released to go back to work. In the fall of 2001, the young couple purchased their first Harley Davidson! The red-and-black ultra classic was given the name Gabriel. Monty had been known for resurrecting the dead, but the 1984 Aspencade was destined for Honda Heaven. While tinkering with the wrecked bike, he had been reminded of one resurrection he could never forget.

RESURRECTING THE DEAD

Monty, Tammy and the boys were headed to East Texas on vacation. Monty and Tammy had discussed the fact that they needed two vehicles. With the extracurricular activities with the boys, Monty couldn't leave Tammy without a vehicle anymore. So they had come to Diana, Texas to resurrect Betsy. Betsy was a 1975 Dodge Dart that belonged to Tammy. She had the vehicle when they had met, but it had been left in Diana after they got married. It had since been moved to the garden and parked in "deadline row." Deadline row is that place where all the family vehicles sit side by side. It is that place you put your vehicle when it is considered to no longer be useful. Everyone knows a "deadline row" when they see it. Normally, it is located with a family member who has some acreage where he can have his own "junkyard." Eventually, that is what happens to the vehicles; they become a pull-your-own auto parts store.

With a phone call, Tammy learned that Betsy hadn't been touched since it was moved to the garden. It was driven back there under its own power. When Tammy told her husband that it had been driven back to the garden, he looked like a little boy that was just told he could go to the candy store. Some of the family members dropped positive comments, which only added to the excitement of getting started.

When they arrived at Dale and LaRece's, they felt like they were actually home. In a way, they were. The trailer house that Tammy was living in when they met was on the same property, and they were still making payments on it. So, they were home, sort of anyway. They visited with the family, and shared what had been happening in their lives since they had been together the last time. It was so nice to leave the rat race of the military and spend time with the family.

The next day, Dale walked back to the garden with Monty, and the closer they got to the vehicle, the more work was obviously needed. The poor thing had four flat tires and all were dry-rotted, with the rims settled deep into the ground. It was impossible to see underneath the vehicle. Dale volunteered some information on some really cheap used tires. That became the first priority. Get the car jacked up and tires removed, along with the fuel tank removed and drained. The longer Monty worked on it, the more serious he got about making it run. It had been running when it was parked there. That was a really good incentive; to be able to actually drive the dead back to El Paso, Texas. That was the goal. If they could get the car back to Fort Bliss, Monty could work on it while driving it daily to work, leaving Tammy with Ole' Blue.

Tammy came back to the garden and brought Monty a cold beer. She smiled when she saw her car blocked up with all the tires missing. She was Monty's biggest fan and had confidence that he could do just about anything. There were plenty of times if it wasn't for her animated confidence in him, he would probably have not attempted many things. That unyielding confidence she had in him was a huge motivating factor in a lot of his accomplishments *[Genesis 2:18]*. They talked about the odds of driving Betsy back to Fort Bliss while they stared at the fuel tank, sitting in the sun.

Two days after starting the project, Betsy was sitting on the ground on four used tires with about 10,000 miles of tread left and the fuel tank re-installed. Monty was tightening up the battery clamps on a borrowed battery. If Betsy did come back to life, then they would invest the money in a new battery, but funds were sparse at the time.

It was getting dark, and Monty wanted to hear the ole' girl fire up before quitting for the night. "You about got it?" Dale asked. Monty jumped with a fright and turned to Dale, "Yes sir, just about." Monty finished tightening up the battery, and said a quiet prayer as he slid into the driver's seat of Betsy. He massaged the steering wheel, as if to try and coax her into starting on the first try. "Ok, girl, it's time," he said as he looked out at Dale, "Fire in the hole." He turned the key and Betsy's engine turned over quickly, but did not start. A quick check determined that no fuel was making it to the carburetor yet.

Monty gave Betsy a small drink of fuel from a coffee can. He stroked her steering wheel again. "Ok girl"; he turned the key, and she fired right up and ran for a couple seconds really rough before dying. You could see the hope in his eyes and when he looked at Dale, he had that old glimmer in his, too. "She wanted to start that time," he said with a snort. Monty nodded and motioned for Dale to stay clear as he turned the key again. This time Betsy turned over quickly, but didn't fire up. "Ok girl, I will give you one more drink." Monty gave her another drink of fuel with his coffee can. Dale watched as Monty turned the key, and again she fired to life. But it was short-lived, maybe a second or two. Monty started to give her another drink, but found that she had fresh fuel from the fuel tank. "I wonder what is wrong with her?" Dale asked. Monty shook his head as he realized it was just about too dark to see well enough to work on her anymore. "I don't know Dale. Would you crank her over for me while I take a look at her?" Monty asked.

Monty wanted to curse the darkness but realized he had been at it since daybreak, and it was time for a well-deserved break anyway. Dale sat down in the driver's seat, and Monty said a quiet prayer. He motioned he was ready as he placed his hand on the throttle and choke linkages. He was hoping to keep Betsy running this time. The engine fired up right away and ran just as rough as the first time, then died. It was dark enough now and about time to head in to the house. The mosquitoes were attacking them! Monty didn't add any fuel. He turned off the flashlight and said one last quiet prayer; "Help me, Lord." He opened his eyes and said, "Ok, Dale." Dale turned the key, and Monty was just looking at the dark engine compartment. As the engine turned over and over, he'd seen what looked like little static-like electricity dancing throughout the entire engine compartment! "STOP!" he yelled! "STOP!" Dale jumped out of the car and quickly was beside Monty, "What happened? What is wrong? You ok?"

Monty realized how loud he had yelled; he replied, "I'm sorry, Dale. I saw something!" With the flashlight on now,

Monty inspected the engine compartment. The sparkplug wires were all touching each other and very moist from the engine oil and gunk. Monty did karate chops at the mosquitoes while picking up small twigs. "Dale, I want to try one last thing before we go in." Dale chuckled, "Sure, with those sticks?" Monty nodded, "Yes, sir. I think the wires are oil saturated and the spark wires are all touching!"

After placing a small piece of twig between each wire, the theory was ready to be verified. Dale took his place in the driver's seat and waited. He couldn't see Monty, but he knew he was probably praying for Betsy to start. Dale said a silent one as well. "Ok, Dale, crank her up," came the command. The slant six 225 engine turned over and started running like a new engine! Dale didn't have to flutter the accelerator. Dale reached up and turned on the headlights! They both came to life, penetrating the darkness.

Betsy was sitting there, idling, and the two men were staring at their work when Tammy walked up with a cold beer. "Honey, I knew you could do it," she said. Monty smiled with triumph, and he took the beer and gave his bride a kiss. "I couldn't have done it without Dale's help." The dead had been resurrected!

[Wow! Right? But don't miss something here. The very thing that I was about to curse, and decided not to, is what showed me the little sparks between the oil saturated wires! Yes, the darkness! Have you ever been mad at something or a situation, and later realize that the very thing you were upset about is what brought you an answer? (Proverbs 14:29) Just something as simple as having to go back to the store for something that you forgot only to run into someone that you really needed to see! I am sure many readers can relate to that. Next time your trials or challenges leave you in darkness, thank God for the darkness and for him to let his light shine through it, Amen?

Now, that is not all. This next part is even more powerful. You ready? Those saturated sparkplug wires on that slant 225 actually have a good spiritual message too! Have you ever belonged to a local church where it seemed like every time something was going to get accomplished, someone else in the body caused problems? Then, the next thing you know the wheels quit turning, and whatever was about to happen for God's Glory stops! (The engine didn't start!) I see those heads nodding up and down. What is happening is that brothers and sisters in Christ that have been called by God to do one thing wanted to do something else. So when a youth ministry program is about to take off and Glorify God, a person thinks they should be part of that leadership but really aren't. Are you getting this? Then when the children's ministry program has a revelation from God for a new program, another person thinks they should take control of that. The analogies can go on and on and on, but you are getting this. I can just tell. But, you are cocking your head to the side like a little puppy, thinking, "Yeah, but I don't see how a slant 225 that wouldn't start has anything to do with that!" You see, the sparkplug wires all have a job to provide fire to one cylinder, with that cylinder being their "ministry." Without the wires doing their job and only their job, the engine won't run! In this case, the wires were "jumping" into the other "ministry fields," which did two things. First, they were not doing what they were supposed to be doing where they were "called" to be. Second, they were causing problems in the "ministry" they jumped into! I love it! Thank you, Lord, for using oil saturated wires for a short message on "Stay where you are planted!" (Read 1 Corinthians 12)]

PRAYERS ANSWERED OFTEN REQUIRE FOLLOW-UP

In October of 2001, Monty and Tammy attended the CMA Rally at Iron Mountain near Hatfield, Arkansas that year. While on a scenic ride and going through Hatfield, Monty noticed a biker talking to someone and making gestures at his bike. Tammy had mentioned needing to stop, so Monty did a couple turns and backed his bike up to the curb, just a few feet from the man. Tammy went inside, and Monty went over to speak with the biker. His discernment had been correct; the bike wouldn't start. The man didn't have any tools, so Monty pulled a couple from his tool bag and removed the seat. The man was another brother in Christ and was also going to Iron Mountain. Monty didn't find anything specific that could be causing the malfunction, but said, "Let's pray and see if the bike is ready to start." The man agreed. They started to pray. Monty couldn't help but notice that they had a small audience.

After a quick prayer, "Lord please fix this bike, you know what is wrong with it," the man pushed the starter switch and it fired right up! They both lifted their hands to the sky, thanking God for his touch on the old Harley! Monty checked the charging system with his multi-meter, and it was good. As Monty installed the seat, he explained to his brother in Christ that the battery could be the culprit and to get it checked while he was still in town. The man smiled and said, "It has been fixed. Brother, there is nothing to worry about." Monty smiled and nodded to the man as he mounted his iron horse and rode off. Monty thought to himself, there is still a reason it didn't start.

* * *

Monty and the family were getting ready to head to El Paso, Texas. They were excited and a little worried as well. Betsy was running and should make the trip, but she had a small transmission leak. Monty assumed it was a seal that would need to be replaced, which is the normal problem for a vehicle that has been sitting for a long time. The trunk was loaded up with a few gallons of water, engine oil and transmission fluid. Tammy followed Monty as they headed west. The transmission was spitting out about a quart every 150 miles, but got worse. Monty thought he had enough transmission fluid, but was wrong. They had started pulling over every fifty miles and putting a whole quart in. Tammy had to follow further and further behind because the transmission fluid was misting onto her windshield.

Then the end had come. Monty and Tammy had already talked about the fact that if Betsy didn't make it, they would abandon her on the side of the road and let her become State property. Well, the time was almost on them. Monty poured the last entire quart of transmission fluid in and shook his head to Tammy. "We tried, Babe." She nodded and patted his arm, "Just pray."

Tammy got back in the family station wagon, and Monty got in Betsy. Adam was in the back seat, "What's wrong, daddy?" Monty replied, "We need to pray that the car makes it home." After a short prayer they took off, knowing they had no transmission fluid left and that they had almost 100 miles to Van Horn, Texas. The transmission didn't start slipping at fifty miles like it had been. It was still pulling good at sixty miles. Monty rolled into the first gas station they came to at just under 100 miles and left the car running as he ran inside. He knew that it would be best to leave the car running and add the fluid, which would help cool down the transmission. They only had three quarts of transmission fluid, and he bought all three quarts. He ran back to the car, opened the hood, and the first check showed the transmission fluid to be at the full mark! Monty checked it again and a third time. The transmission was full. It had not used a drop in the last nearly 100 miles! After putting the three quarts of unused transmission fluid in the trunk, they took off. Betsy did not use another drop of transmission fluid the rest of the trip to El Paso, Texas. What a miracle!

Monty worked on the car and fixed up major things during the next year, to include getting her inspected and legal for the roads. Betsy became his everyday commuter while Tammy had the newer vehicle. After nearly a year, they were getting loaded up to head to east Texas for a few days before Monty would be driving Betsy to his Basic Non-Commissioned Officers Course (BNCOC). The day before the trip, Betsy started leaking transmission fluid! Monty crawled underneath the vehicle, and the transmission was covered in fluid. A quick trip to the wash rack and all of it cleaned off, then a short trip home to see where the leak was. Again, the entire transmission was covered in fluid! Monty just couldn't believe it. After a whole year, the car starts leaking again. Then he reached up and checked the sending unit; it was finger-loose! He couldn't believe it! The transmission sending unit was the culprit. It was an easy fix, and the transmission never leaked again!

> *[Sometimes we pray for God to help us out, and he does. BUT he also wants us to follow-up, Amen? I have lost count of how many brothers and sisters in Christ will pray for God to get them through a storm. God answers the prayer, and then they allow the next storm to happen by making the same decisions that led to the last storm! It could be anything, maybe finances. You ever done that? A financial storm comes, and you are unable to pay a bill and pray for God to help. The financial blessing comes, and then you make the same decisions to buy the same things that you really didn't need that leads to the exact same storm in another month or two. Many a drunk (to include myself) have prayed at the porcelain throne, "God, get me through this and I will never drink again." God answers your prayer; you do live, even though you were sure you were going to die; BUT, you are back in the bar drinking before you know it. God wanted you*

to follow-up. Yeah, I got my T-shirt for that one, too. After God answers a prayer, also follow-up by asking God to show you how to avoid the same storm again, Amen?]

A WASTE OF TIME PREACHING – OR WAS IT?

The rally master asked Monty if he would give the message Sunday morning. This was the first time that Monty was being asked to preach the message on Sunday morning at a rally! He was excited and intimidated at the same time. Monty assumed since Dennis was the current president of the chapter that he would be giving the message. But, after a few minutes discussing it, Dennis told Monty to go ahead and give the message. Monty and Tammy made a trip home to get the materials needed for an object lesson. The next morning, even though there were over 200 chairs set up facing the stage, only about 30 of them were occupied. The night before, every chair was taken and people were standing up watching the show. But today, when the man on the stage is going to talk about Jesus instead of the secular activities, the crowd was much smaller.

This was Monty's big debut as the "biker preacher." Monty preached an object lesson called "The Refined Christian," and was done in 30 minutes. There was no decision for Christ, and only a couple of folks patted him on the back. But that didn't stop folks from asking him to share Jesus with them at other rallies here and there. In the back of his mind, he had written the Bell County Expo message off as a "failure." Eventually, he forgot all about that particular message, except on occasion when he would look over his previous messages for one to give again. That one he had kept, but never felt like preaching it again since it obviously hadn't touched anyone.

* * *

Over a year later, Monty pulled up at Kay's in Nolanville, Texas after a nice scenic ride with some friends. He dismounted his iron horse and as he was removing his helmet, he heard, "There is the wild preacher man!" Monty assumed whoever was speaking that he was referring to one of his friends he was riding with. He placed his helmet on the mirror and looked up to see a man headed in his direction. Monty smiled at the stranger, who said, "What's up, wild preacher man?" Monty looked behind him and then back at the stranger. The man had his hand out, when still 10 feet away, ready to shake his hand as if some long-lost friend. Monty put his hand out; they shook hands and embraced. The man squeezed hard and patted him on the back, "How you been, wild preacher man?" Monty looked at the stranger, "I am blessed, brother, and you?" The stranger smiled, "You don't remember me, do you?" Monty felt terrible inside as he nodded in acknowledgement. "No sir, I am sorry, I don't."

The stranger patted Monty on the shoulder, "You changed my life, preacher man!" Monty felt worse! Here is a man he couldn't remember, and yet he had made a major impact on the man's life. The man laughed aloud, "I am just a lump of coal, but I strive to be a diamond every day." The words pierced into Monty's soul. Those words could only mean one thing. The man must have noticed the realization in Monty's eyes, "That is right, sir. Your message about whether I am a lump of coal or a diamond ring changed my life!" Monty was still in shock as he realized that the message he had written off as a failure was, in fact, used by God to change at least one person's life.

[Whenever we are obedient to God, and especially when we step out of our comfort zone for Jesus, the devil will do everything he can to make you believe you are wasting your time! I had decided not to re-use a message that had changed a man for God's Glory! No, he didn't raise his hand at the service, but yet he was changed and lived a different life from that day on! I want you to

realize that when you are doing something for God, it is NEVER a WASTE! You tell the devil to shut up! He is the father of all lies and will get you to believe it (if you let him)! Why did God wait so long to give me a confirmation? Maybe so it would have such a huge impact on me, and I would NEVER forget it, amen? Not to mention put the story in a book so you could see that you are not alone. I promise you, if you are truly doing something for God and for HIS glory alone, it is not in vain! Amen? (1 Corinthians 15:58)]

A CALL FROM THE PAST

In the winter of 2001, Monty was on the computer when an instant message from someone that he thought would never have anything to do with him popped up! She claimed to be his ex-wife's daughter! "How could this be?" he thought. His pulse quickened as he thought about his long-lost princess. They had not seen or been in contact since 1986! It had been 15 years since her mother had left him for another man. He quickly typed a reply on the instant message box. He was afraid that this was a trick. Even after all these years, he prayed that his ex-wife had changed, but he had reason to doubt that she had. He was always wondering what she might try next, even after all these years. The last attempt to try and ruin his life was a close call.

Guilty Until Proven Innocent

Monty returned from lunch to the motor pool. As he walked into the office, his motor sergeant was anxious. "You need to go to the CID office right away!" Monty laughed and started to blow it off, but in a matter of minutes he realized that his boss, along with the entire office staff, were serious. He was at a complete loss as to why any CID special agent would want to see him. He drove over to the headquarters and walked in the front door, ready to get to the bottom of the situation. A CID agent met him and asked if he could help as he looked at Monty's name tag. As Monty started to introduce himself, the agent said, "Right this way, Sergeant Van Horn." Monty followed the man back to the special agent that wanted to see him. The agent got up from his desk and said, "Follow me, sir."

Next thing he knows, he is standing in front of a set of ink pads and getting his finger prints, palm prints, closed fist prints taken! Monty asked what this was all about and gave an awkward laugh when the man was short; "We will get to that, sir." When all the prints had been taken and Monty was sitting in a chair facing the special agent sitting at his desk, the interview began. Monty was still completely at a loss as to why he was here.

Then, it all made sense when the man asked his first question, "Sir, do you know a Lesley...?" Monty sat back in his chair in shock. "Of course I do. She was my stepdaughter years ago. Why?" The man had an iron, solid face; "Sir, have you ever physically or sexually abused Lesley?" Monty laughed nervously, "Of course not! What kind of question is that?" Then Monty got serious; he thought, "Oh no. Something has happened to his little princess!" At least she used to be his little princess. "Is Lesley ok? What has happened?" The guy didn't even blink; "Fine, sir. She is fine. I have a sworn statement from her that you physically and sexually abused her!"

Monty was in shock! "Wait just a minute. When is all this supposed to have happened? I haven't seen Lesley for years. Her mother has put her up to this." The special agent made it clear that the sworn statement was all the proof needed, and that SSG Van Horn was going to be spending a long time in prison.

His visit with his lawyer was short. "Sir, you are guilty unless proven innocent in this case." Monty could not believe this. It was simple; the lawyer explained that since the girl had signed a sworn statement that, as far as anyone was concerned, it happened. That is the end of it. Monty was still in shock as his lawyer said, "Look I can see that you must be innocent." Monty frantically nodded his head; "Yes, of course! I love my princess. I would never hurt her in any way." The lawyer said, "Then what you need to do is get out of the Army as fast as you can. Bring this up in a civil case because here, you are guilty until proven innocent." Monty thought about his ex-wife. How can there be so much hate, he thought to himself. He had way too much time left on his enlistment, and there was no way to get out early.

Monty asked a question that gave a possibility of winning this unwinnable battle. It was a slim chance, but he had to make a phone call and find out if he was going to prison, or if he had a chance to beat this fabricated nightmare he was now living. As he drove back home, he had so many emotions flowing rampant. His little princess had signed a sworn statement stating that he had hurt her! What bothered him the most was that if Lesley signed the statement, then does she really believe her own lies? Could his ex-wife have actually brainwashed his little princess to believe that he had done such awful things to her? He cried as he pulled into the drive at his home. He was going to make a call tomorrow, and it would decide his fate!

> *[The call was made. Praise the Lord that the man (ex-in-law) was willing to speak on my behalf to the CID. The evidence he had, and the statement he made during his visit with them, was enough to get the CID to re-investigate charges. Everything came back unfounded.]*

* * *

Monty sent the last instant message, "Let's talk on the phone," and sent her his phone number. The phone rang in a minute. After 15 years, he was actually talking with his stepdaughter. They talked for about an hour and, at times, the conversation was emotional for both of them. The bottom line was that she had to talk to him because her therapist told her that she needed to. Her husband had also told her that it was time to get on with her life and encouraged her to call Monty. They closed the conversation with a commitment to get together soon. Monty was planning on heading up to Kansas within a couple weeks.

In fact, Monty and Tammy made that trip, and had a good time visiting and spending the night. Monty helped make a "snow family" of little snowmen with Lesley's children. Monty and Tammy also joined the family to watch Auburn, Lesley's daughter, play a basketball game. She scored two points right at the end of the game!

While there, he also got to talk to his biological son, Richard, on the phone for the first time in 15 years. The highlight of that conversation was a comment from Richard; "You are more religious than I thought you would be." Monty chuckled, "That doesn't surprise me." He had reached a point in his life that he didn't even try to guess what may or may not be said about him. He was sure of one thing. None of it would be good. The couple headed back to Texas after the-two day visit, promising to make another trip soon.

VACATION ON THE HARLEY

In the summer of 2002, Monty and Tammy headed out on vacation. They had a stop scheduled in Kansas. They had the 2002 Ultra Classic and their camper in tow. It was beautiful riding weather. After a night in Cap Rock Canyons in Texas, the couple rolled in at Flagstop Resort and RV Park in Milford, Kansas. Lesley, her husband, Aaron, and the children were there to meet them. They got camp set up, and had a great time visiting and reminiscing about the past. Lesley made the comment, "It seems like most of my fondest childhood memories are when you were in the picture." She would ask questions about a vague or small portion of a dream or "vision," trying to see if Monty could explain some of it.

"Do you know anything about a Shell Island?" she asked. Monty grinned as he remembered taking her and her brother on a pontoon boat to "Shell Island." He had told her and her brother that they owned an island, and it was full of shells. They would get their sand buckets and, after a few minutes on the water, land at "Shell Island." She interrupted his thoughts, "You do!" He nodded, "Yes, it is a small island at the Toledo Bend Outdoor Recreation Center we used to go to. I would get you guys all excited about this 'Shell Island' and take you two there so you could get a bucket full of shells!"

They sat around the fire and visited until it was time for bed. It had been a great time, but it was time to head on to Indiana.

After two days in the saddle, the couple pulled in at Dick and Paula Van Horns' place in Otterbein, Indiana. After the initial hellos and hugs, Monty and Tammy set the camper up.

Some of the local folks checked out their camper as they set it up. It never failed that people would be amazed that what they had behind their motorcycle was a camper. Monty and Tammy were inside visiting with Paula when Dick, Monty's Dad, entered the house. "I need to show you guys something." He was obviously concerned about something! He waved quickly, "Come here; this is not good." Monty and Tammy followed Dick outside. He pointed to the top of the tree that their camper was parked under. "You have to move the camper!"

Monty sighed as he looked at the huge dead limb right above their camper. He looked at Tammy, and she said, "Did you pray about where to set up?" Monty nodded, "Yes Honey, I always do." She looked at Dick and said, "He prayed; it stays there," and she walked away, leaving Dick stunned in silence and Monty with an uncomfortable grin on his face. "I did pray, Dad."

Dick shook his head in disagreement. Monty knew that his dad would worry the rest of the time he was there, so he asked him where he wanted them to move the trailer. Dick showed him a spot on the other side of the house. Monty told him that maybe he could get Tammy to move the trailer tomorrow, but today it was going to stay where it was. Dick wasn't happy, but had some hope that they would move it tomorrow.

The next day, Tammy and Monty were looking at the clouds moving in. They were at a ballpark north of Otterbein. The wind was picking up, and it looked like they might get wet! Monty's dad asked them if they were going to stay. They wanted to keep watching Britny, Monty's niece, playing soft-ball, but decided to head back to the house. They got on Highway 52, heading back to Otterbein, and the storm was obviously already where they were heading. Monty took his time, trying to miss the heavy rain. They actually pulled in the drive still dry. There were some puddles of water in the drive and yard. They had avoided getting a single drop of rain on them. God is good!

Monty got himself an O'Doul's and sat down on the porch. He and Tammy were sitting together while Monty played the guitar. Then, a couple neighbors walked up and said, "Sir, we will help you get the limb off your house if you want us to." Monty was silent and still trying to comprehend their statement. The two young men must have seen the confusion on his face. "Sir, you have a tree limb that has fallen on your house." Monty looked at their camper, still standing, and looked up at the dead limb. The young man commented, "The other side of the house, sir." Monty followed them around to the other side to see that a perfectly healthy limb had been broken by the high winds, and landed right where his dad had said would be a safe place to move the camper. The limb appeared to have been twisted off the tree and then leaned up against the house.

> *[Praying about the little things is important too! My wife had total peace about staying under a dead limb, simply because where to set up was prayed about and I had received peace to set up there. The look on Dad's face when he returned home from the ball games was priceless. I didn't have to say, "I told you so." He studied the freshly broken limb lying against the side of his house. You could see he was thankful that we had not moved the trailer. Do you pray about the small things or just the "important" things? Most of us only ask God to provide divine wisdom when we don't feel adequate to make the decision on our own. It's a shame, but I am just telling you the truth, Amen? God loves it when you pray about the little things too (Philippians 4:6)].*

OPERATION IRAQI FREEDOM/ OPERATION ENDURING FREEDOM

In March of 2003, Monty was doing something he thought he would never have to do again! When he had left the Army, he never thought that he would ever be going back to any hostile land. But now, as a Bradley Fighting Vehicle (BFV) Field Service Representative (FSR), Monty was at home packing his duffle bags. He was not looking forward to going into harm's way, but he loved his soldiers and knew this was where God was taking him.

Monty flew with the soldiers from the 1/10 CAV of the 4th Infantry Division. The vehicles were inspected and re-inspected, with every minor deficiency worked off, and the fleet was ready to roll out. Monty would speak about the Lord openly, and nearly no one seemed to mind. It is amazing how "tolerant" people become towards the "religious" ones when they are in need of comfort. In the evenings before getting some sleep, Monty would be reading his Bible, and there would be a soldier asking him questions about something they had remembered from their childhood. Monty would smile, put his Bible down and start explaining or, in most cases, finishing the story for them. One such case was a young man asking if he was mistaken, but he thought there was a story in the Bible about some handwriting on the wall. Monty enjoyed going over chapter five in Daniel with the soldier. Another was about some guys being tossed into a furnace. Again, Monty got to read and go over Daniel, chapter three. Then a soldier asked, "Didn't one of the disciples get swallowed by a whale during the storm?" Monty smiled as the soldier finished, "Was that the same storm when Paul or some guy walked on water?" The field of harvest was ripe. Very seldom did a night go by that someone didn't have a question for Monty. It brought back memories to Desert Storm.

B.Y.O.B.

SSG Van Horn was sitting on his cot, with nearly all of his maintenance team sitting around on cots, with three to four men to a cot. There was an MRE case cover that was hanging outside on the entrance to their GP Medium tent that read B.Y.O.B. in large letters. When you got closer, you could read below those letters "Bring Your Own Bible." The K troop 3/3 ACR Maintenance team had a daily Bible Study in their tent every evening before turning in. It was amazing how all but a couple of his men were responsive and participated in these Bible Studies. Monty felt then that the Lord was tugging at him to become a preacher or teacher. God was performing miracles when they prayed, and soldiers were touched by the Holy Spirit!

One night during their fellowship in the Word of God, SPC Hayes had a migraine. He told SPC Hicks, "This headache is killing me." SSG Van Horn placed his hands on Hayes' forehead and said, "In the name of Jesus, be gone!" The look on Hayes' face was priceless! "It's gone! Hicks! My headache is gone!" SSG Van Horn sat down on his cot and stared into the "fireplace." It was all made out of MRE boxes, and the artwork by some of his men had made it really nice. He looked at the painted flames, trying to absorb what had just happened. Quite a few folks started talking about the miracle. Word got out about SSG Van Horn's "magic hands." Monty would laugh and say, "It is all God!"

> [God gives us a glimpse of what he wants to do through us long before we are truly walking along the path HE wants us on! As we look back, we can see things that happened that were confirmations from God, then, of what he wanted us to be doing for HIM! That was the first healing **from God** during a prayer from me and from that day

*on, I took prayer much more seriously! Before,
I had tried to use eloquent words to make sure
I was getting God's attention. He doesn't care
about that! He looked into my heart and knew
that I knew he could heal Hayes (Read Matthew
21:22)! And he did! Today, I have been called the
"drive- by healer," because I quit trying to impress
anyone and especially God! It is not uncommon
for me to simply lay my hand on, or even point
to the requested spot, and say, "In the name of
Jesus, be healed." But physical healing of people
is not the limit of God!]*

* * *

At Camp Udari, with only a day or two left before rolling
out, Monty was being asked to look at another Bradley with a
turret drive malfunction. When he arrived to the back ramp,
the soldiers cringed, "Great! You will climb into the turret
and there won't be anything wrong!" Monty laughed, "That
doesn't happen all the time." After climbing inside the turret
and flipping up the turret power switch, Monty began to pray
over the vehicle. While the vehicle went through its start-up
built-in test, he thought of how their comments were similar
to what he had heard for years. Even during Desert Storm.

* * *

SSG Van Horn was walking past at least five, if not half
a dozen, men standing behind one of the K troop tanks. He
stopped to see what the trouble was. The tank team, lead
by SGT Ramirez, explained that they couldn't get the quick
disconnect for the generator on. SSG Van Horn was getting
impatient with the explanations that were coming from every
person in the group. "It's just a quick disconnect. Put it on!" he
snapped. Ramirez, his right-hand man grimaced; "Sarge, we
have been trying." Monty had not worked on tanks before but,
now that he had become the motor sergeant, was responsible
for them as well as his Bradley Fighting Vehicles. "What do

you have to do if you can't get it on?" he asked. Ramirez stated that they would have to pull the power pack.

After getting an explanation of what he would be feeling and how the connection should work, he was asked, "You want to try?" He shrugged his shoulders. "Why not, let me see." As he reached down into the hull and felt the steel line, he slid his hand to the quick disconnect they had described. "Hey, Sarge, this is not a Bradley! SSG Van Horn, your magic ain't going to work on these."

Monty felt the connection click in place, and a quick tug confirmed it was together! As he pulled his hand out, he smiled, "Ok, I think it's on." They started laughing. "Right, Sarge, just like that!" SGT Ramirez thrust his arm down into the hull to check. The look on Ramirez's face confirmed that it was installed and secure. This tank had been a nightmare to the tank mechanics for hours. Not only that, but this was either the second or third generator that they had put on the tank. As they started talking about his magic, Monty walked away and said, "It is a God thing, guys. It's a GOD thing."

Later, the news came that the tank still wasn't charging. SSG Van Horn went back over to the tank and, after getting a detailed briefing on everything that his tank guys had done, he could find no reason for the tank to not be charging. SSG Van Horn was leaning on the front slope with SPC Hayes and SPC Hicks. Monty looked at Hayes, "I think we need to just pray for it to start charging!" Hayes was the first to agree! He was probably thinking about how his headache had disappeared when prayed for. The driver looked at the trio, "What are you all doing?" SSG Van Horn looked at the driver, "We are going to pray for your tank." The three soldiers laid their hands on the front slope and prayed. It was a simple prayer; "Lord, please fix this tank. Amen." SSG Van Horn looked at the driver and said, "Start her up and get her out of here." The driver shook his head and started up the tank. The astonished look on his face confirmed that their prayers had been answered. God is so good!

[That tank didn't have another charging problem for the duration of the war. We serve an awesome God! So many times, we think we can only pray

for God to take care of physical healing or spiritual things and leave the huge worldly problems to ourselves to fix! It doesn't matter if it is a tank or some spacecraft, our God knows its design! Amen? Where do you think we got the design? Now a decade later, I am still praying for God to fix vehicles!]

* * *

Finally, the turret was fully powered up, and Monty traversed back and forth and checked the elevation as well. He exercised the launcher. Everything was working just fine. He climbed down from the turret. "We told you that the fault would go away!" Monty laughed, "It's a God thing, Guys!"

A MESSAGE FROM A SOULLESS BIRD.

Within a few days, the 1/10 CAV was no longer in Kuwait; welcome to Iraq! Monty wondered if he was really where he needed to be. Doubt entered in, and he entertained that maybe he had made the biggest mistake in his life. Did he really need to be in a thin-skinned HUMMER, with a blue flak jacket on that was screaming "shoot me; I'm a contractor"? The progress had slowed down to a snail's pace as the unit entered the outskirts of Baghdad. Then the unit went into a herringbone formation, and Monty could hear small arms fire! His driver, SPC Alonso Ortiz, dismounted the vehicle with his weapon, leaving Monty to think really hard about the situation he was in. "My God! Why in the world am I here?" he thought to himself.

There was a huge explosion not too far off and the ground shook. The small arms fire became more intense with yet another smaller explosion, which still vibrated the ground. Monty started assessing the ballistic integrity of the canvas door he was leaning against, and realized he was really in a mess! He spoke from within himself, "Hey, God! It's me! Your servant! Yeah, just checking to see if you realize what kind of mess you have me in here?" *(Deuteronomy 31:8)* Monty felt like balling up in a fetal position and lying on the floor, but he was way too large to accomplish that. The next explosion was the loudest, and the canvas door recoiled and the material popped with a CRACK! Monty looked around in dismay. "Lord this has to be the biggest mistake you have made! Do you really know what is going on here?"

Monty was having such a pity party for himself as a bird flew across the front of the top of the hood of the HUMMER. Monty watched the bird land next to a puddle. He stared at the small bird and watched its reaction to the next small explosion. It cocked its head over, as if to make an assessment on whether to stay at the side of the puddle or leave. Monty watched the bird get a drink from the puddle. And then suddenly, it snatched up a small worm! Then it was as if the bird looked right at him. Even though birds don't smile, it was like he did smile before taking off with his meal.

Immediately, Monty felt the Holy Spirit touch him! This was a simple, but powerful, message from God! It is an old message, too. Monty thought about how the sparrows are not as important as he is to God, and that the Bible says that God even cares about and provides for them *(Matthew 10:29-31)*. Monty felt the Holy Spirit swelling up inside and he suddenly thrust open the canvas door, stepped out of the HUMMER as another string of small arms fire could be heard off in the distance. He walked around the vehicle and stood next to his driver. SPC Ortiz looked at him, startled. "Sir, what are you doing?" Monty smiled, "Standing next to you." SPC Ortiz shook his head, "You ain't got a weapon, sir." Monty laughed; "I know. If they hit me, I will be with Jesus. But if they hit you, I will have a weapon."

[I had let the devil sow a seed of doubt! I entertained that seed to which I became scared. Fear is of satan and paralyzes us from accomplishing God's work! I became irritated with the "fact" that God had me in a mess I was not supposed to be in! God didn't shake the ground or scream at me audibly! He sent a sparrow! I pray for the reader to see through the storm they find themselves in, and for God to provide them a "sparrow" to see and learn from. Also, notice that God didn't "speak" to me until I shut up and quit complaining. May that "soulless bird" bring you comfort today.]

After what seemed like forever, they were loaded back up and moving again. They drove past the aftermath of another unit that had already been through the city and utterly destroyed the enemy. Only small pockets of resistance were popping up here and there. The city reeked of death. Vehicles were smoldering everywhere. One stretch of road, which they had driven on, had what seemed like hundreds of warehouses! Monty noticed that every third warehouse was destroyed. He told his driver, "You realize that every third building is flattened?" His driver nodded, "Yeah, so?" Monty smiled, "We are telling them that we can do what we want when we want and they can't do anything about it!" His driver did not seem to understand the impact of the statement. Monty explained that psychological casualties and the wounded are better than just killing some of the enemy. It totally breaks down the enemy from within themselves! He explained that the wounded and the survivors will realize that the wicked evil ones from America own the sky, and can reach out and take out anything they want whenever they want. It was obvious that a lot of fierce fighting had occurred, and nearly every vehicle was that of the enemy. After hours of traveling, they had seen less than a handful of American vehicles. What a blessing that God had protected the US troops, and that the Holy Spirit had gone before them! This made Monty think about that prayer his chaplain said, over the net, before they headed into Kuwait during Desert Storm.

* * *

The moment that no one really wanted to see was here! The day that all of them had been trained for was just around the corner. SSG Van Horn was in the TC (Track Commander) hatch of his maintenance 113 as the lead vehicle for the K troop maintenance team. The 3rd squadron was lined up for movement. The fear was that Suddam and the Iraqi army would use biological weapons on them! The wind was still blowing into their faces, and that was the perfect weather conditions for the enemy to use nuclear biological or chemical (NBC) weapons on the Americans with the least amount of complications for themselves! That had been small talk for days. Every soldier had donned their NBC gear time after time, making sure they were fast and that it worked! The radio crackled; it was the squadron chaplain, "Let us pray." While the chaplain was praying, Monty felt moved to open his eyes and he noticed that there was a milky, white substance low to the ground, about 50 or so feet from the front of his vehicle! He reached for his mask, but felt a sudden peace come over him and he relaxed. What he saw he could not understand. It was like a heavy, white gaseous mass that was slowly floating towards them! But there was no worries; Monty felt a total peace, and started wondering if anyone else could see what he was seeing. The internal communication system broke in on the prayer, "Hey, Sarge, uh, do you see what I see?" Monty was staring at the white, lethargic substance getting closer. "Uh, Sergeant Van Horn?" Monty snapped out of his trance long enough to depress his internal communications switch. "Yes, I see it, Hicks." Monty looked at Hayes, who was standing in the cargo hatch with his weapon, and he nodded at SSG Van Horn. He was seeing this mysterious substance too! The Chaplain was asking for a hedge of protection and that the Holy Spirit would go before them and protect them, and that they were giving the battle to God. When the Chaplain said Amen, the wind stopped! The substance hovered for a second or two, and then the wind began blowing on their backs! The substance disappeared moving forward before them! "Wow! Please tell me you two just saw the same thing I did," SSG Van Horn said over the intercom. "Oh, yeah!" was their excited reply.

> *[What an awesome testimony of God's love and compassion, and his providing of a visible confirmation that he was with us! When we asked others if they had seen the Holy Spirit go before us, we found no one else! I still want to cry when I think of how God allowed us to see his presence at the battle! It was a modern- day 2 Kings 6:14-17 confirmation! I wonder if there were actually Iraqi tanks destroyed by "tanks of fire"? Well, we know it is possible.]*

65

CALLING HOME

The unit had been on the move for weeks. They would stop and set up a temporary area of operations, and then in a day or two be headed out again. Monty had been in the cavalry himself and knew this would probably be how they would spend the entire year. He knew that even when the other units might start setting things up, like back in the real world, that the saying "scouts out" would have an impact on him also. One thing he knew was that God had him here, and it was for him to let his light shine for his Lord, Jesus Christ. Monty was thankful for everything he had, and was especially grateful for the benefits of being a civilian contractor. Monty had an umbilical cord to the real world. It was something he couldn't tell anyone about because then, they would want it too. People have been killed for less, so it was easy to keep it a secret. It was an iridium satellite phone!

What a true blessing to be able to hear his wife's voice once in a while. He had talked to her less than a week ago, but on April, 26, 2003, he had a yearning desire to call her. He figured it would go away and he would wait for another few days at least. The company didn't want the FSRs using the phone more than they really needed to. The desire became overwhelming, and he couldn't get the thought out of his mind. Monty took his CVC bag and went inside the small tent that had been provided for him. Gary Hatch, Monty's battle buddy, had one just like it too. They couldn't sleep in the tents because it was too hot, but they would store their gear inside the tent to give them more living space on and near their hummers.

Sitting on the small folding chair, he powered up the phone and waited for it to "boot up" and find a satellite signal. Then he dialed Tammy's number. When the call finally went through and started ringing, Monty felt anxious. He couldn't wait to hear her voice. "Hello?" It was his wife. "Hey Babe, I love you," he said. That was usually the very first thing said because it was not uncommon for the phone to lose its signal, and they would get cut off. After a couple seconds delay, he heard her voice. "I love you too." She sounded depressed. They both were not ecstatic about being apart, but they knew it was in God's plan. But she sounded worse than the last time they had talked. She sounded like she was crying!

"Are you ok, Babe?" he asked. Tammy tried to hold back the sobs. "No, Momma passed away today." Those words sent a jolt through his entire body! The tears didn't swell up and then overflow from his eyes. An emotional dam behind his eyes somewhere opened up, and two rivers of tears gushed out as he started crying. "I am so sorry, Babe!" He tried to quit crying and asked if she wanted him to come home. After blurting the question out, he wasn't even sure how he would be able to get back home. They were still on the move. But he knew there had to be a way. Tammy didn't hesitate with her answer, "Oh, no, Baby! I mean, I would like for you to be here, but I don't want you to try and get back for this."

Monty shook his head. "But I can come home. I just have to find out how to get back." Tammy was adamant and reminded him, "Baby, you and I both know where Momma is. You keep on doing what you need to there. I will be ok!" Monty nodded in agreement but couldn't quit crying. "I will call back when I can talk, Babe." She said ok, and then he hung up the phone. Wiping his eyes so he could read the display on the phone, he powered down the iridium.

Once Monty had regained his composure, he went to talk to CW3 Kevin Johnson. While visiting with Kevin, he learned that there was a process for getting back to the states, but it would be an arduous journey. While Monty was checking out the options and Kevin offered to get more information, Tammy was thanking God for the phone call and the strength he was giving her. She couldn't believe she told him to stay in Iraq! Maybe his call was what gave her the strength. Out of any other time that he could call, God orchestrated for him to call within half an hour of when she had received the news that her mother had passed away. That wasn't some coincidence! God was saying, "I am in control of all things." Tammy was strong! She had confidence. She realized this was not of her, but from God. She hoped she hadn't hurt Monty's feelings by telling him to stay, but she didn't want him trying to get back and be in harm's way either.

Monty left Kevin's "hooch" and had to find his brother in Christ, Larry Dabeck. Monty knew he needed some prayer to get through this, and his brother in Christ was the man he needed to find! It was a quick search. Larry was standing next to his hummer, eating an MRE. Monty briskly walked towards his brother, feeling the grief and helplessness building up again. Larry could see something was wrong and after a short and emotional explanation, the two men held each other and Larry prayed. Monty got his composure back and went back to his tent after getting his CVC bag from the locked storage box. Monty was able to talk to Tammy for about half an hour, and then he told her he would call back tomorrow. He knew he wasn't supposed to, but he knew he needed to. Then the next phone call was to his superior, and he informed the man that his mother-in-law had passed. Monty provided the address that Tammy would be at, expecting her to receive flowers from the company. She didn't....

> [Have you ever wondered about God's timing? I know I have many times. I have heard the saying, "God is never in a hurry, but he is always on time." God moves us to do things at a specific time because he knows all things. Amen? (Ecclesiastes 8:6)]

MOTHER'S DAY FLOWERS

On Saturday the 3rd of May, 2003, the unit was at another location. This one was supposed to be for a few weeks, if not a couple months. You could look in any direction and see desert for as far as you could see. With the unit setting up for a long campout, the civilian contractors consolidated their vehicles and equipment together. Gary Hatch, George Malone, Ken McCall and Monty had all their hummers backed up to each other with a tarp setup, providing shade. Gary was working on a tank part while Ken was reading a car magazine that was being passed around from person to person. Monty had a wild idea! "What if I could get a flower shop to deliver some flowers to my wife for Mother's Day?" he thought. He had a credit card. The challenge would be that the iridium phone stay connected the whole time!

He was talking with his wife daily since her mom had passed. He didn't talk more than 5 minutes, and told her that he would call just about every day instead of waiting and talking longer. He went inside the blistering hot tent. The temperature outside the tent was close to 110 or more! The guys all had bottles of water, inside an old sock hanging from the mirrors on their vehicles, and would douse the sock about every 10 minutes. They hadn't had any ice since they left Kuwait. The hot desert breeze blowing onto the socks and the water evaporating would cool down the water inside the bottle to a tolerable drinking temperature.

As soon as Monty slipped inside the tent, he heard Ken, "You have got to be kidding me!" George remarked, "Dude! You better take a bottle of water with you, or you will dehydrate in a minute!" Monty waved them off as he lowered the flap. All his buddies knew he was getting ready to use the phone, and that was the only way to keep it a "secret." Standing out in the open desert with an iridium phone would be like taking candy to a day-care!

By the time the iridium had powered up, Monty could feel the sweat rolling down his neck. It was stifling hot in the tent! He had looked at his watch and knew if he was going to get flowers ordered, it was now or never. He dialed the number (1-903-555-1212) and waited, hoping he had remembered the right number for operator directory. Monty heard total silence and was certain he had been disconnected again! Then he heard a click, "What city, please?" Monty snapped, "Longview, please." The lady with a monotone voice replied, "name of person or business?" Monty replied, "Flower shop, any flower shop." The lady stated, "Casa Flora?" and Monty said sure. "The number is 903-..." Monty wrote the number down furiously as the number was said, and then there was silence. He thought maybe he was being connected, but he had been disconnected.

He was pretty sure he had written the number down correctly and repeated it to himself as he read the number. He started dialing the number to the flower shop and could feel his heart pulse getting a little faster. He was sweating profusely! He punched in the numbers 903 and as he looked down at the paper for the next set of numbers, sweat rolled off his nose and landed directly over the last four numbers! The ink became a black blur on the paper immediately! "Oh, no!" he thought as he punched in the three he just read and then quickly what he thought the last four was.

While he waited for the connection, he wiped at the blur, hoping he would be able to confirm that he had input the correct numbers. The blur just smeared across the paper, totally obliterating any evidence that there ever were any numbers there! "Great!" he thought. "Casa Flora," a lady answered. Monty sighed, "Yes, ma'am. I want to order some flowers for my wife." The lady was very polite. "Sir, we are about to close, so your order will not be delivered until.." Monty didn't hear the rest. He couldn't believe his dream was about to be shattered! He gasped, "No! Please! I am in a tent in the desert in Iraq. I really want to get flowers to my wife, please!" The lady replied, "Sir, I am sorry, but we are closing the store in a few minutes and we don't have anyone to deliver the flowers."

Then she must have realized what he said. "Sir, did I hear you correctly? You are in Iraq?" Monty sighed, "Yes, ma'am, inside a tent in the desert in the middle of nowhere on a satellite phone in Iraq." It was quiet on the other end. Monty could feel the dream dissolving as the conversation continued. "Sir, where were you wanting them sent?" He didn't miss the "were wanting," which is in past tense. He knew she was just being nice. He had waited a few minutes too long. Monty sighed with disappointment. "It's a place outside of Diana." The lady at the other end screamed at someone to wait! Monty could hear the lady talking to someone that was leaving for the day. It sounded like this person lived in or near Diana! He pressed his sweat-soaked ear hard against the phone, trying to hear their conversation. He could hear her relaying the information that she was talking to a soldier in Iraq. He thought how ironic to be referred to as a soldier, but then just how many contractors were living in the desert?

"Ok sir, we might have a plan here. Where do you want the flowers delivered?" Monty gave the address. "69 Christie Road, Diana, Texas." The lady repeated the address to her co-worker. He heard the co-worker telling her that she didn't know where that was, but she would take the flowers to his wife. His pulse was going so fast now and so hard that his neck was twitching with every heartbeat! He could feel it spasm with each beat! After giving the lady the directions, she asked what kind of arrangement he wanted, and he simply replied, "I can't be picky under the situation; whatever you got available." Then she asked for the credit card information. Then there was static and the phone went silent!

"Oh, no way!" he thought. It could take anywhere from five minutes to sometimes you just have to wait until another time in the day to make another phone call!

He looked at the display in disbelief and saw that it indicated he was still connected. His sweat dripped onto the display as he heard a faint, "Sir?" He couldn't believe it! He quickly answered, "Yes." She asked again, "Do you have your credit card information?" Monty provided the information, and she let him know that a co-worker that lives near Margie would be dropping the flowers off on her way home. He had done it! He calmly thanked her, but inside was doing summersaults!

When he opened the flap of the tent, it felt like an air conditioner was on. The 110 degrees was like a 30-degree drop! Monty was so happy and had to share with his buddies what he had just accomplished. Ken McCall shook his head, "You have just made us lower than whale doo-doo." Monty snatched his bottle of water hanging from the mirror and started drinking it as he took a seat to watch the sun set. He smiled to himself, thinking, "Tammy will be so surprised."....

> *[God, again, set the perfect timing of the call (Jeremiah 29:11). He also had the operator pick the flower shop that had an employee that lived a few miles from Margie. He provided a good connection with the phone that normally would have been disconnected in that amount of time. Do we serve an awesome God or what?]*

..... Tammy was at her sister's, getting ready to go to town. she, Margie and Apryl were going shopping in Longview. The phone rang, and Apryl picked it up. "Hello?" The voice on the other end was not what or who Apryl expected. "I have a flower arrangement for Tammy Van Horn and wanted to be sure someone will be home." Apryl turned and looked at her Aunt Tammy, who was looking in the mirror making sure her hair looked ok. The lady on the other end of the phone said, "Hello?" Apryl snapped out of her thoughts, "YES!" she snapped. Tammy looked at Apryl. Apryl calmed down. "I mean, yes ma'am there will be." She turned her back to Tammy and lowered her voice, "May I ask from who?" The lady replied, "Richard Van Horn." Apryl gasped, "Ok, thank you!" Margie came down the hallway. "Well, we better get going..." Apryl met her in the hallway, and the two disappeared to the master bedroom. Apryl explained that Uncle Monty was sending flowers to Tammy!

It had only been about 15 minutes since the phone call, and Tammy was ready. "Ya'll ready to go to the store?" Margie and Apryl looked at each other at a loss for what to do! Suddenly

Margie got up and rushed to the bathroom. Tammy followed after her to the bathroom. "Margie, you ok?" Margie replied that she would be ok, just an upset stomach. For the next 30 minutes, Apryl and Margie made excuses for not leaving until finally the car was seen coming down their drive.

Tammy was actually in the bathroom when the lady was at the door. The duo had her come in and told her that this was perfect timing. They were like three high school girls waiting for Tammy to return to the kitchen. When Tammy entered the kitchen, she saw the "delivery lady" standing by the door with her sister and niece. Then she saw the huge arrangement of flowers and exclaimed, "Oh, Margie, they are beautiful! Did Bennie or the kids get them for you?" Margie shrugged her shoulders. "Good question. You're the closest; you tell me." Tammy started reading the card and as she realized they were hers from Monty, she trembled and her knees became weak. She felt faint, and the chair was just close enough for her to plop into. As she sat down, she started crying. Apryl couldn't hold her tears back either. "I have always loved Uncle Monty, but now, I love him even more." Apryl went on about how her uncle went to a lot of trouble to show his love for her aunt. "He is such a romantic." She sighed and wiped her tears away.

GOING WITHOUT MAKES US APPRECIATIVE

The 1/10 CAV did stay at that same location for quite some time. They actually made portable outhouses. This was the first time in four months that they had a "private" place to use the bathroom. That was the big talk of the whole area of operation. The "three-hole" latrine was talked about and treated like the most precious thing in the camp. In fact, when the time came to break camp and move to the next location, maintenance personnel actually loaded up the "three-holer" to take with them.

> *[It seems to be human nature to take everything for granted! It probably seems comical to some readers about taking a three-hole outhouse with you. But some readers are nodding north and south, saying, "been there, done that and got my T-shirt." When you go without, it doesn't matter what it is; you realize how important it is. That is why God allows us to go without sometimes. How could we ever be so thankful for the porcelain throne if we don't go without it? Just saying....]*

* * *

(A couple months later) The 1/10 CAV arrived to Camp Caldwell. Monty and Gary were living in high cotton now. They were parked on concrete and had a building to seek refuge in. For months they had been traveling with the unit in the desert. They had been living on their Hummers since day one. For the first time in over three months, they had their first experience of having ice. There was rumor that they would be having a hot meal for the first time in over three months also. The thought of actually having a hot meal and ice water was beyond description. The rumors continued. The mail would be catching up, and they would be receiving a couple trucks full. There was going to be a "mini-PX" for them to actually purchase items. Monty and Gary took all these wonderful pieces of news and filed them in the back of their heads. They figured there was no reason to get their hopes up. Besides, they were happy for their ice water! *(Philippians 4:11)*

> *[Isn't it amazing what we take for granted? I just have to reiterate here. You never think about thanking God for the things you have readily available. Honestly, when is the last time you thanked God for the roll of toilet paper you have? You don't. You can always find someone talking about what brand of toilet paper they would rather have. It is the same with water.*
>
> *When I first returned from Iraq, I was happy to have endless amounts of ice-cold water. Yet, I would hear people complaining about how one brand tastes like dirt, or that another brand came from filter processing plant instead of a natural spring. When you spend over 90 days in the desert with a bottle of water inside a dirty sock hanging from the mirror on your vehicle, you don't care about the taste, or where it comes from.*
>
> *You will find yourself thanking God for the breeze that is lowering the temperature of your water. You find yourself thanking God for the two bottles of water you received that day! Is the water cold after a couple times of saturating the sock and God drying it out with his breath? No, but it no longer scorches your tongue either. When the water supply was short, we didn't have*

*the luxury of wasting water to pour on the sock!
When we were rationed to two water bottles a
day, we would just add MRE coffee to the water.
Who wants coffee in 120 degrees? No one does.
But we would find ourselves thanking God for
the instant coffee to help make the hot water
taste better.*

*Have you ever seen the little wad of toilet paper
you get with an MRE meal? When was the last
time you thanked God for the toilet paper on the
roll next to you? When was the last time you
thanked God for the cold bottle of water you
are drinking? Hmmm, I thought so, just another
thought to ponder. We serve an awesome God,
don't we? By the way, you probably inhaled
about ten times while reading this and guess who
provided that? Just saying....]*

With the mission slowing down and the unit staying in one
place for a while, the mail did catch up, and Monty received
a few Christian Bible Studies and documentaries as well as
movies! In a day or so, soldiers were coming over to Monty
and Gary's "hooch" to watch a Christian movie. The movies
sparked up questions. And the next thing you know, there is
a Bible Study two days a week at "Monty's place." The number
of soldiers that attended the Bible Studies varied, depending
on the mission. After over a decade, God has Monty in harm's
way giving Bible Studies again! He didn't have a B.Y.O.B. sign
and they weren't meeting daily, but God was trying to tell him
something.

*[If you find yourself making a "360" in life and
you are doing nearly the same exact thing all over
again, stop and ask God what he is trying to tell
you. You ask, "why?" Because he is trying to get
you somewhere you didn't end up the last time
around. Amen?]*

* * *

Boom, boom, boom. Monty stirred in his cot. "Get up! Monty, get up!" Monty rolled over in his sleep, oblivious to the sounds again. "Boom, boom, boom..." The voice was even louder, and others were yelling. Monty stirred a little and awakened with a start. "Boom, boom, boom...." Monty looked over, and Gary was standing inside the doorway of their building, waving frantically. "Come on, man! Monty, it's a firefight! Get over here!" Monty rubbed his eyes and looked again. Gary was standing just inside the doorway in only his drawers. At the moment that he realized Gary was screaming at him to join him inside the building, he saw tracers. "boom, boom, boom...." Monty looked at the tracers, looked at the soldiers positioned at the corners of the building, and realized he couldn't do anything more than what the trained soldiers were already doing. He waved back at Gary and rolled over, and went back to sleep as he sighed a simple and soft, "Protect us all, Lord." (Read Proverbs 28:1.)

Monty slept the rest of the night until his biological clock snapped him awake at 0430 hours. Gary was in awe at Monty's lack of concern. He asked questions like, "What were you thinking? Why didn't you come inside the building? Weren't you afraid?" Monty smiled. "I couldn't do any more than what was already being done." Gary shook his head. "One stray bullet, man, and you could have been dead!" Monty laughed. "Yep, a stray bullet inside the building or outside the building. Besides I would have been with Jesus." Gary decided to talk about something else. Gary really didn't care or mind Monty being a "Jesus Freak," as long as he didn't try to get him in the conversation. Monty smiled at his silence, but wished he could get Gary to talk about Jesus. Gary would make occasional comments, insinuating the questionable sanity of Monty. Monty would just chuckle and think to himself, "If he only realized the power of my peace and comfort comes from Jesus."

[Just for the record, it was learned later that it was only us firing rounds anyway. See, I didn't lose any sleep and didn't need to (Psalm 23).]

DO YOU REALLY TRUST ME?

A few days later, it was time for Monty to make a trip to one of the Observation Posts to check on a couple vehicles with transmission issues. When the vehicles marshaled up that morning, there were only three vehicles making the trip and only one was a cargo hummer! The lieutenant told Monty that she needed him to be the rear vehicle, and she would assign a M60 gunner to his vehicle. Alonso looked at Monty, and it was clearly written on his face that he did not want to be the last vehicle in the convoy of three vehicles! The enemy had been hitting either the first or last vehicle of convoys, and then showering them with small arms fire. Monty wanted to tell the young lieutenant that he was not going to go, but that small still voice inside asked, "Do you really trust me?" He simply looked at his driver, who was anticipating him to say no. Monty turned to her and said, "Ok, but we have to make room." Alonso looked shocked but with mixed emotions, the two worked quickly at converting the cargo vehicle into a rear security vehicle with gunner.

The last stop was at Camp War Horse, where some supplies were procured and Monty got to visit with Bill Graver from General Dynamics. Bill was stressing out due to daily mortar attacks on his camp. Monty said a quick prayer and listened to more than one account of the near misses that Bill and some of his co-workers had undergone recently. Monty gave Bill a quick handshake and hug as they lined up to leave again. Bill noticed he was the last vehicle. "You are the rear guard?" Monty smiled, "Yep." The look in Bill's eyes was that of fear. Monty and Bill were friends, and had been for some time.

Monty was concerned about the stress his friend was showing, and prayed to himself for God's favor and protection over him.

Monty was still thinking about how shook up Bill was while staring at the hummer in the middle, about 75 meters in front of them. "That is the vehicle we should be in," he thought. CW2 Craig Coger was in the middle vehicle. The dust cloud enveloped them in a split second! As the cloud grew bigger, you could see in slow motion that both doors were blown wide open! Monty and Alonso had saw all of that in the split second before the deafening sound from the explosion reached their ears! The hummer in front of them had been hit! A solid concrete building block, same size as a cinder block, was flying in the air right towards Monty! It was turning over, end over end, heading straight towards Monty, and he knew it was going to hit him. The block was floating in the air slowly, but at the same time rapidly approaching the passenger's side of the windshield! Suddenly the entire vehicle was shifted to the left lane of the road. The vehicle did not swerve or veer into the left lane. The vehicle shifted instantly from the right lane directly in line with the solid block to the left lane! Monty and Alonso watched the block fly past them and then in an instance, they were inside the cloud of smoke and gasped for a breath as the "gun powder" smell overwhelmed them! Everything was like a slow motion silent movie. There was no sound!

Monty opened his door and stepped out on the ground. He looked at Alonso, and his driver was looking in shock at him! Monty realized as he watched Alonso lifting up his right leg and slamming down towards the brake that they hadn't stopped yet! Without any effort, Monty reseated himself in the vehicle until it came to a stop! Monty stared at the ground outside to verify that they had stopped. Everything was still silent and in slow motion! The ground quit moving and the sound came back. Monty stepped out onto the ground and was less than one arm's-length from CW2 Coger's vehicle. Their vehicle would have collided right into the rear of Coger's vehicle if it hadn't shifted into the left lane! Monty ran around to the passenger side, and Craig was sitting in his vehicle, slightly slumped over.

Monty said, "You know it is by the Grace of God you are alive!" Craig twisted and pulled a piece of paper from his pants' cargo pocket. With shaking hands, he handed Monty a written copy of Psalm 91. Monty smiled as he patted his brother in Christ. "Yes, you do know." Monty found the driver fully alert and standing watch, waiting for the small arms fire to start. Monty repeated his thoughts to the driver, "You know it is by the grace of God ya'll are not hurt." The driver replied with a shrug, "Whatever," and kept watching for the first sign of small arms fire. Up ahead was the lieutenant's vehicle. She turned around and was heading back at a high rate of speed.

The next few minutes was consumed doing a quick damage assessment of the vehicle, and strapping down the broken doors and other canvas pieces that were torn from the vehicle. The enemy did not fire a single shot at the small convoy. Either it was a solo IED plan or God just stopped them from engaging the Americans, but not a single shot was fired. The convoy continued back to Camp Caldwell, but with a couple friendly Apaches leading the way in the air.

> *[Have your plans ever been changed? Have you ever found yourself being given a decision to make that you know you don't have to do, but down deep you know you should anyway? We didn't have to be the rear vehicle. I could have refused, and the lieutenant knew that, and during our conversation said she would understand if I refused to be the rear vehicle. That is probably why Alonso expected me to say, "No, ma'am, I'm staying here." Maybe God provided a female lieutenant so I would stand up and be a "man." Lord knows I couldn't cower down and go home with my tail between my legs, since a young lady was leading the convoy! You men reading this know what I am saying!*
>
> *Now, in case you didn't catch it, I got out of a moving hummer. I stepped on the ground! But, that is impossible! I guess I must have stepped on the back of one of my flying angels! When we returned back to camp, I had Alonso write out everything that happened. While he was doing*

It, he suddenly stopped and looked at me. Then he asked me a simple question that I could not answer. He wanted to know how I got back in the vehicle. Maybe I was actually standing with my foot in the palm of the angel, and he lifted me back into the hummer? I don't know. What I do know is that I stepped out of a moving hummer and got back in without any problems. That is a God thing! Amen? (Read 2 Samuel 22:3-4 and Psalm 34:7)]

By the time the three vehicles arrived back at Camp Caldwell, everyone knew about the near miss. Gary was part-battle buddy and part-mother hen, asking Monty questions about what happened and if he was ok. Most of the folks had headaches, with Craig having the worst one, as well as some loss of hearing. Gary gave Monty some medication for a headache and the two of them talked. Monty got to share more about how Jesus helped out and how the hummer was moved over as well as him getting out of the vehicle, but "something" helped him back in. Gary soaked it all in. It was obvious that Gary was glad to see his battle buddy back in one piece.

It was almost time to lay down for the night when CW3 Johnson approached Monty. "we need to go look at a couple transmission issues at Bravo troop tomorrow." Monty nodded, "No problem, Kevin." Kevin filled him in on what time they would be leaving in the morning and then headed back to his own area. Gary was fidgeting. "Monty, you are going to go outside the wire tomorrow?" Monty chuckled, "Of course." Gary explained that he thought Monty should take a break, since he had a near miss today, but Monty wouldn't listen. He replied, "Gary, they need their vehicle fixed. You want to go look at it instead?" It was quiet for a minute. "Goodnight Monty." Monty smiled up at the stars as he laid back, looking up at the canvas painting of stars that God had provided for him. He went to sleep, thinking, "and God knows the names of every one of those stars..."(Psalm 147:4).

The next day, as well as the rest of the trips that Monty went outside the wire, went without incident, thanks to the Lord.

REQUEST IN THE MIDDLE OF THE NIGHT – BAD NEWS

On the 30th of July 2003, late at night, Monty stirred as he heard a soft voice, "Monty." Monty tried to make the voice go away and just about drifted back to sleep. He heard the voice just a little bit louder again, "Monty, you awake?" Monty opened his eyes, but it was pitch dark. He rubbed his eyes to be sure and listened again. He couldn't see who was asking him if he was awake, but he had his eyes wide open. "Yes, I am now. Who is it?" The voice answered, "Sergeant Zorn. I have some really bad news." Monty sat straight up in his cot and felt the mosquito net touching the top of his head. "I didn't want to wake you up, Monty, but this is really bad." Monty could tell by the quivering voice that the young man was having a hard time! "It's ok, Scott. What do you need?" The young motor sergeant must have taken a deep breath, and then said everything in one long sentence. "Lieutenant Nott has been killed, and my maintenance team is taking this hard, as well as me, and the chaplain is on a mission, and I hate to ask you, but thought you might want to go be with the guys right now since the chaplain is not here." Monty was still stuck on "Lieutenant Nott has been killed..." "Sure I can go over there, what happened to Lief?" The answer didn't matter. The bottom line was that 1LT Lief Nott was dead.

Monty had broken bread with Lief, and they had talked in fellowship about their common bond and their love for Jesus. Lief was active in a youth ministry back at Fort Hood. Monty thought about how Lief would just beam when talking about the ministry. Monty was dressed in a flash, brushed his teeth and walked over to the Alpha maintenance team office. Every one of the mechanics was awake and in the office. SFC Zorn gave Monty a handshake and hug. "I can't believe this." Monty nodded in agreement. "I am so sorry Scott."

Monty spent the next hour or two just sitting with the team. The men spoke very little about their leader. 1LT Lief Nott was a respected leader, and they all loved him. Everyone was in shock about what had happened. Monty also learned that SGT Mickey Anderson and SPC Emily Deavers had been shot as well. Monty and Mickey had talked on more than one occasion about the motorcycle ministry. Mickey was also interested in riding for the Lord when he got back home. Prayer was offered and received by some, and Monty went back to his area. Monty just couldn't believe he had lost a friend.

*[I have been with many brothers and sisters in Christ that have told me they didn't go to those in need because they didn't know what to say or do. Please listen. Many readers need to hear this! **JUST GO!** Don't say anything or do anything if God doesn't have you. The **ministry of presence** is something not taught a whole lot, but your presence is more powerful than you will ever know! JUST GO! (Read 1 Thessalonians 5:11.)]*

GOING HOME ON BREAK–
EMBARRASSED OVER WEAKNESS

Finally, the time had come for Monty to go home for a 90-day break! Monty had coordinated with Tammy for a brand-new bunkhouse to be purchased. It had been delivered and was at the farm waiting for him to put it together. Monty was telling Gary about his new toy, and he couldn't wait to get home to put it together and go riding. He explained that the bunkhouse is the camper of all campers for a biker. It is pulled behind the bike, and when you get to your destination, you fold out the bed and tent portion and have a king-size bed with a nice living space! The couple had paid for every option that was available!

When Monty shared with Gary what his plan was, the look was priceless. Gary had a blank stare. He couldn't compute any logic at all out of what Monty was explaining. After what seemed like forever, Gary spouted, "You really need your head checked!" No matter what Monty tried to tell him about the difference of camping in a bunkhouse with the wife and being where they were, Gary would wave him off as if to say, "Talk to the hand." Monty laughed, "Come on Gary, take me over to the airfield and let's see what is leaving tomorrow."

The battle buddies drove over to the building where the communications for the helicopters was at to get more information on any flights scheduled to go to Camp Anaconda. While they were in the area of the helicopter, they saw MAJ Tetu! Monty smiled as he seen the brother in Christ headed towards him. "What's up, Brother?" he said as the two did a handshake and hug. "I'm going home for about three months,

Mike." Monty stated. MAJ Tetu smiled bigger. "I am happy for you, brother. Wish I could fly you there myself, but my heeleee-chopter is broke-ed." Monty laughed, "I wish you could too, Mike." A quick goodbye and a "if I don't see you before you leave" speech, and the two shook hands and hugged again. Monty watched Mike walking away, thinking about how the man had seen the worst of him come out nearly six months ago, but yet still loved him like a brother.

* * *

"Here, hold this for me. I will be back," The warrant officer said, leaving Monty holding the CVC bag. Gary and Monty watched some of the squadron leadership walk up the hill, disappearing into the darkness. They sat down on their duffle bags and other gear with the soldiers around them and waited. They were on their way to somewhere, but didn't have a clue where that was. They were near the port where the unit would be getting their vehicles soon.

After quite a while, Gary and Monty saw the warrant walking back down the hill in a hurry. "Come on, let's go!" The two picked up their duffle bags and gear and followed him. It didn't take more than 100 or maybe 200 steps at the most before the two contractors knew they were not going to be able to keep up. They looked at each other, then back at the warrant that was at least 50 steps ahead of them. He turned around and seen the slackers. "Come on!" Monty and Gary didn't stop walking but they couldn't walk any faster with all the gear, and the warrant, with just his CVC bag, eventually disappeared into the darkness! The two started saying some things back and forth, and Gary was letting loose some expletives, but more than normal! Monty was getting even angrier with every step, but assumed that when they reached the crest of the hill they would see the inconsiderate and uncompassionate man waiting for them. They were walking adjacent to a line of "T-walls." ("T-walls" are huge but portable concrete walls used for protection against enemy mortar attacks.)

Sweating profusely, the two battle buddies made it to the crest of the hill, and it was all they could do. The man was nowhere to be found! What they saw was unanticipated. The

85

road went on as far as they could see and the "T-walls" continued forever. The "T-walls" were set up with about a 30-inch gap between each one. On the other side of the "T-walls," the two could see a "tent city" was set up, and it went on forever as well. They looked at each other without a clue of where they were supposed to go. The two abandoned men sat down on a "T-wall" next to each other in silence. Neither one of them could believe the situation they were experiencing. They looked at each other, and Gary rattled off another string of expletives. Monty was fuming. They both just sat there and watched soldiers walk by and hummers drive by.

The sweating had slowed down and the heartbeat was getting back to normal when a hummer stopped suddenly as it went past them only a few feet. "Hey guys, how ya'll doing?" It was MAJ Mike Tetu. Monty had broken bread with this brother in Christ. They had shared what God was doing and had done in their lives. Mike could see something was wrong and got out of the hummer; his jovial self! Mike was always happy, and that was something Monty admired about the officer. Even when Mike had a full plate, he would be smiles and just keep on going. Mike looked at Gary and then back to Monty. Then it happened! Monty let loose every expletive that he knew and hadn't said for years! While he explained their predicament in the most candid yet tactless method, the eyes of MAJ Tetu widened! It wasn't until Monty finished that he realized that he had lost complete composure! He felt his face burning with fire from the flow of blood flushing his face. *(Read Proverbs 29:11.)* MAJ Tetu was still in silence, making an assessment of his friend who was obviously livid.

Monty's shoulders slumped in defeat as he realized what he had just done. "I am sorry, sir." Mike reached over and put his hand on Monty's shoulder. "It's ok. Just hold on a minute." He went to his hummer and told the driver, "Meet me back at the tent." He reached down and snatched up Monty and Gary's "A-Bags" effortlessly and said, "Follow me guys," as he slid through the 30-inch gap into tent city. Monty and Gary followed the Major through a maze of tents. In just a few minutes, they were inside Mike Tetu's tent. "Have a seat, guys, I will be right back." Mike went over to some other soldiers and got some information on tent vacancies.

When he returned, he was his happy self. "Ok, got you guys in Charlie Maintenance Team tent, which is the closest one to where the trucks will be dropping off your 'B-bags.'" The Major picked up the bags again, and Monty protested, "Please, sir, I can get my bag." Mike shook his head. "Nonsense, follow me" and off they went. The walk was a short one, and they both had a spot to put all their gear. "Ok, guys. Sorry, but this will have to do," he gestured towards the "T-wall" right next to the tent. "'Your "B-bag' should be on the next truck, and it will stop right there." He pointed at the gap a few feet from them. Monty was humble and humiliated still, and quietly thanked him. "Thank you, sir." Mike smiled from ear to ear; "Not a problem, guys!" He walked briskly back towards his tent and the two watched after him.

* * *

..... They watched Mike walking towards one of the heli-copters. Monty looked back at Gary, who was studying his flushed face. "You ok?" Monty realized he was embarrassed about losing his composure over six months ago. "Yeah Gary, I'm fine! I just can't wait to go home!"

> *[The person you think you can count on is not always and, in fact many times, is not the person you can really count on. The person that really cares and helps out may be the person you haven't even given a second thought. It may be that person that has too many things to do to help you anyway! Many times it is the person that has more responsibilities and tasks than any other around them. The one that has a servant's heart, that is the one you can count on. Oh yes, many times it is a person that doesn't have any respon-sibility to help you at all that will help you. Why? The servant's heart comes from a relationship with God. The more intimate we are with Jesus, the more we are like him. Mike didn't have to stop, let alone stop, to ask about our situation and then take time out of his schedule to help*

87

us. Mike was on a mission. He stopped what he was doing to help. Mike is a servant of God. The other guy? Well, he will be the first to tell you, "I look out for number one." Was I mad? Yes, at first but, again, God allows all situations for us to learn how to be better servants ourselves. Which person are you? Spend a few moments with God before reading any more. Which person are you and which person do you want to emulate?]

"THERE ARE THESE HARLEY PEOPLE HERE"

Monty was free. The trip back from Iraq went without any issues, and he was home. He was in the saddle of his 2002 Ultra classic with his wife, enjoying the open roads of Texas. The bunkhouse was back at the Chapter T-fest campgrounds, set up and the air conditioner going. Yes, air conditioning was one of those differences that Monty had tried to explain to Gary. Monty had told his battle buddy back in Iraq that it wasn't the same, but Gary wouldn't listen. To Gary, the idea of camping after being in the Iraq desert for months was crazy. The ride had been a beautiful one and they were headed back to the Chapter T-Fest to enjoy the rally with friends. The couple was just about to get on the loop and head back to camp when the Harley started wobbling real bad! Monty was able to get Gabriel slowed down and to a stop safely. They had a flat! Monty was happy that they were only about three miles from the Temple Harley shop. Monty knew they had less than an hour before the shop would be closing, but it's "Harley Family," he thought.

The phone call was a slap of reality right to the face! "Sorry, man. we don't make house calls," the man snorted. Monty felt betrayed. "I am only three miles from the Harley shop." The piercing words of reality will never be forgotten. "Sucks to be you." Monty shared with Tammy about their "Harley Family" and then called his brother in Christ, Dennis Ng. Dennis was the current Warriors of the Way president and a man with a true servant's heart. "I will be there as soon as I can, brother; just relax," Dennis stated.

While the couple was waiting and still soaking in the final comment from the local Harley store, a young lady stopped to check on them. She asked if she could help out in any way, offered to get them some water. Monty and Tammy said that they were ok and had help on the way. She insisted on calling her parents that didn't live but a few minutes away. Monty told her that she looked familiar as she made the call to her parents. "There are these Harley people broke down," she said. Monty snickered to himself. "We are Harley people alright," he thought. She got off the phone and was oblivious that Monty had heard what she had called them. They visited for only a few minutes, and then a car pulled up. And to their surprise, it was Bill and Louise Seale. Now Monty knew why the young lady looked so familiar. Bill and Louise belonged to the Chapter-T family! They rode a Goldwing, thus their daughter's comment about "Harley people."

[Isn't it amazing how often the ones that we expect the most from are the ones that let us down? That is because we set them at a higher level of expectation! I was expecting more out of the "Harley Family" then the "Rice Burner" family. I have no doubt that is why God let me hear her say, "These Harley People"! That was a spiritual slap in the face. Life is not about who we are, or what we ride! It is not even about where we are riding to! It is about who we ride with and the ride we take. Amen? Who have you been riding with lately? (1 Corinthians 15:33) What kind of ride have you been on? Think about it. That is what life is about. Just saying....]

Bill and Louise were also going to go to the Chapter T-Fest. Dennis arrived in about an hour with his trailer, ready for some action. After taking the Harley to the Ng's residence, Dennis gave the stranded couple a ride to their home to pick up their own truck. As Dennis reminisced about one particular event, he mentioned how many times the group had to stop frequently due to different challenges and ailments all the people in the group had. He chuckled, "I guess you could call us the geriatric crew." Marcy started laughing when he said that.

Monty didn't know what the word meant and immediately asked, "Geriatric?" Dennis nodded and started to continue his story. Monty asked again, "Geriatric?" Dennis abruptly stopped, "Yes, geriatric." Just as Dennis started to continue the story, Monty interrupted him again. "What does geriatric mean?" Dennis snapped, "Get a dictionary." Monty felt his face flush right away. Marcy sighed, "Dennis! Monty, it means the elderly." Monty chuckled, "Oh, ok."

Dennis continued the story. There was a time that Monty would not ask questions like that, but not anymore. If he didn't know what something meant, he would ask. He thought back to how his pride of not asking a simple question changed the course of his life.

* * *

As Monty walked into the courtroom for the final divorce hearing, he saw his lawyer sitting at the large desk with not a single piece of paper. That seemed odd, he thought. He wondered where were all the copies of the sworn affidavits and the copy of the court transcript of Tammy and her husband's divorce. He sat down next to the lawyer; "You don't have the copies here with you?" The lawyer twisted a paper clip in his hands: "No, sir. We shouldn't need them today." Monty was in shock, but replied, "I have all the original sworn affidavits and the court transcript in here." The lawyer looked at the briefcase Monty sat on the desk. The lawyer excused himself and walked over to Monty's soon-to-be ex and her lawyer. They went to a small conference room and closed the door.

Monty sat there quietly as he looked into the back of the courtroom and saw the young couple he knew had been subpoenaed to be there. The husband was one of his soldiers, and the wife had provided a rendezvous point for the two lovers to spend the night while Monty and his soldiers were on field maneuvers. Monty felt better knowing they were present, even though the sworn affidavit proved adultery. Monty also had a court transcript from Tammy and her ex's divorce, where he admitted his relationship with Monty's ex. The reason Monty had spent the money for all of this was that in Louisiana if a spouse proves divorce on the grounds of adultery, the innocent spouse gets full custody. Monty wanted his son more than anything else.

His lawyer returned, and Monty noticed his wife was crying. Monty felt a sense of satisfaction, but was concerned that his lawyer was alone with them. When he asked what that was all about, the lawyer gave a vague answer. When the big moment came, Monty's lawyer stood up and said that they were filing for divorce on the grounds of "living in concubinage." Monty leaned forward and asked what that meant. The lawyer said, "It's the same thing as Adultery." Monty had a really bad feeling about his lawyer!

As the case progressed, and even though he didn't understand nearly anything that was being said, what he did understand was that everything he had in his briefcase was not permissible as evidence! The word "concubinage" kept coming up. And at one point, Monty felt like he needed to ask the judge if it was the same as adultery! But he let his pride keep him quiet! Instead of getting full custody of his little man, he got joint custody. For some reason, anything that happened prior to their legal separation date was not admissible!

Monty asked his lawyer why they couldn't use any of the evidence he had. The lawyer said, "I'll explain later." Monty learned later that if he would have just asked the judge if there was a difference between adultery and "living in concubinage," there would have been a new trial set, and he would have had a new lawyer! The joint custody thing didn't happen either. His child support check came back every month with no forwarding address available. The address it was going to was his ex-mother-in-law! His ex-wife was in hiding with his son! He didn't even know for sure what state his son was in for three years.....

[I think pride is the number one weakness that satan uses on men (Proverbs 16:18)! We just don't like to admit we don't know something. I mean pride stopped me from simply asking the judge a question. Looking back, I understand that God wanted me to raise my three boys "like

my own," and I did. Maybe I wouldn't have if I had also been raising my biological son. Maybe I would have been telling all three of my boys, "Why don't you be more like Pokey!" I don't really know why God allowed me to be separated from my biological son and for us to really never get to know each other, but I do know that my God is in control of all things and he knows what could have happened. We will never know.

I spent years at Christmas time moping around because I didn't know where my biological son was! From December 3rd (his birthday) until January, I was a bear! Then in 1994, my wife came into the garage and said, "I don't want us to have Christmas anymore. I would rather none of us have Christmas if you are going to be like this every year when Pokey's birthday gets here!" Then something clicked, and I moved on. I am sure my three boys were happy too! That was the first real Christmas for all of them! It is sad, I know, but like I said, I am an ordinary person. I am sure you have parts of your life you would like to delete from your "book" but hey, someone needed to read this. Amen? If this portion of the book ministered to you, please let me know at https:www.facebook.com/ABikerSoldiersJourney.]

FAMILY TIME AT BRUSHY CREEK

It was September of 2003. The ride to East Texas was awesome, and the bunkhouse pulled like a champ. Gabriel, the Ultra Classic, didn't have a problem pulling the camper to Brushy Creek Campgrounds. Monty and Tammy had the camp set up in minutes! The huge advantage to the bunkhouse over the old camper trailer they had was a five-minute set-up versus a minimum 30-minute set-up! The other camper had its shortcomings and could prove to be a challenge for any couple during assembly. They sat in their folding chairs and looked out over Lake O' the Pines. Monty noticed a few people had watched them set up their camper. It would always bring a smile to his face just thinking about what they might be thinking as the bike rolled in with a trailer in tow. "Hey honey, should I offer a nickel tour?" Monty asked. Tammy shook her head violently, "Don't you dare!" Monty chuckled, thinking about their trip to Indiana with the old camper.

* * *

The scenic ride from Texas had been beautiful! They had arrived at Twin Bridges State Park in Oklahoma on their way to Indiana. The entire campground was pretty much shaded and right on the river! It was beautiful! As the Harley made a low rumble through the campground, campers were appearing from their safe havens. Monty couldn't help but smile at the folks and wave to the spectators. They found a vacant full hook-up site that could accommodate the largest Class A motor home built. Monty swerved left and rolled to a stop, facing a couple standing in front of their huge Class A. Monty smiled at them and nodded. They gave an awkward nod back. Tammy unplugged her headset and dismounted the iron horse. It wasn't like Monty needed anyone to guide him back. But it was much easier to back up with the trailer without a passenger.

Tammy walked over to the picnic table, removed her helmet and sat it down. Monty steered the bike backwards down the paved site until it was almost to the end and nearly perfectly level. Killing the engine and sliding out the kickstand with his heel, all in one smooth motion, Monty dismounted his iron horse. Tammy walked over to the cooler, which sat on the tongue of the trailer, and unzipped the cover while Monty placed his helmet next to hers on the picnic table. By the time he returned to the bike, Tammy was drinking an ice-cold water and handed Monty one. He opened it and whispered, "There are a bunch of folks watching us again." Tammy nodded without looking around. "I know, it is always like this. I love this location, Babe." Monty took a long and much needed drink from the bottle. Then he sat the half-empty bottle on the ground and unlatched the trailer from the bike hitch.

The two of them rolled their camper into place, as if they had done it all their lives. Without talking to each other or making any motions whatsoever, the trailer was positioned right where they both knew it would be best and started unloading what they had strapped to the top of the camper. As Monty carried his Ovation guitar in its case to the picnic table, he realized that the spectators had multiplied. The couple had the top ready to be removed. He whispered to Tammy, "I think we should charge admission." Tammy laughed as Monty stood up and started walking towards the spectators. She snapped, "Monty, don't do this."

It was too late. Monty yelled at the top of his lungs for those that were the farthest away to be able to hear him as well. "We charge $5 admission to watch us set this thing up!" Monty heard Tammy groan, and he knew he had embarrassed her. The couple just across from them laughed, and the man walked towards Monty. "I just might have to pay it because, sir, you have got my curiosity maxed out!" Monty laughed and walked towards the man, and they shook hands as they introduced themselves. The man watched as they spent the next 20 minutes putting their home away from home together.

* * *

Monty smiled, still thinking about being in Oklahoma back then, but sighed. "Ok honey." The two just enjoyed each other's company and talked about how God had blessed them so much. By late afternoon, the campsite was full with vehicles parked in adjacent camp sites not being used yet. Dick and Paula, Monty's dad and stepmom, were down from Indiana. Cynthia, Monty's oldest half-sister, and her family, from Jefferson, Texas, had come in to visit. Carla, his youngest half-sister, and her boyfriend were also there. Marty, his little sister, and her family from Longview was sitting next to the picnic table, enjoying the music. It had been years since all four of the children had been together. Dale, Tammy's dad, was also relaxing at the campsite, and her sister, Margie, and husband, Bennie, were sitting in some folding chairs, enjoying the peaceful atmosphere. Tammy's brother, Richard, and his family was also relaxing at the campsite. This was the first time, since Monty and Tammy had gotten married in 1986, that their two fathers finally got to meet each other.

> [Sometimes it takes a major event in our lives to wake us up to what is really important! Spending time with family a long distance (or nearby) away becomes less important as time goes on, until either a tragic event or an event that wakes you up and you realize what you might be missing. Why do we go years without seeing our family that lives a long way off? In many cases, not a long way off! The common excuses are, "We just don't have the money," "We just don't have the vacation time," "We just never find the time." You have heard those before or you have used those before right? We tell our family members we are sorry, but "maybe next year." But, is it really true?

The fact is that we use our vacation for some-thing else or we spend the money for something else, but we could have used it to travel to see our family. The truth is we just choose not to. It isn't until God allows us to go through a hard time or experience a situation in our lives that we realize we may not get to see each other again; then we find the money or we make the time. Unfortunately, we usually wait until there is a funeral to go to. We are all guilty of this, me included.

In this case, my entire family is in the same place at the same time. It had been years since this had ever happened. Why now? Because I had just spent six months in harm's way; the news media was constantly listing the KIAs and I was going back! That is the situation that God used to wake up the family and say, "we need to spend some time together!"

Our priorities are what we make them. Slow down for a minute and think about the last time you took some vacation and went to see some family far-off. Maybe you should put this book down and at least go give them a call, and maybe even start making plans for a future visit.]

Monty and Dick played the guitars, and the younger generation was running around making lots of noise. Monty was relearning names of all his nephews and nieces and placing the names with faces. After hamburgers and hotdogs and a few hours of fellowship, it was time for folks to leave. It didn't take but a few minutes after the first person said they were going to leave that nearly everyone else headed back to their respective homes.

Monty and Tammy were preparing to turn in for the night when they found a pair of shoes that belonged to one of Cynthia's children. At first they were going to just hold onto them, but with a couple phone calls, they learned that the child only had one pair of shoes and needed them for school the next day. So they took the shoes to Cynthia's home in Jefferson. Cynthia's husband had been quiet and distant all day at the lake. He had spent the majority of his time away from the crowd while they played music and visited at the campsite. The look on his face was priceless when he opened the door to their home and saw Monty standing there with the only pair of shoes the child owned. His brother-in-law was holding a cold beer in one hand and a lit cigarette in the other. He smiled uncomfortably and thanked Monty for the shoes. He gave an insincere invite to stay, but Monty politely refused and headed back to the campsite.

[I used to drink and smoke. You learned that in the first chapter. But, I never let my kids go without so I could have a cigarette or a beer (1 Timothy 5:8). Yes, I was mad, and yet sad at the same time. There was nothing I could do or say that would help. If anything, it would make matters worse for my sister and the babies.

My wife and I prayed for a conviction from the Holy Spirit. The more intimate we get with our Lord, Jesus Christ, the more other people become important in our lives and our own personal "needs" become less and less (Philippians 2:4). I started to delete this section of the book quite a few times, but the Spirit of God has made it clear that there will be readers that need to see it! Let me know if you are one of those readers. Since I prayed and received peace from God, I already know that I will receive confirmation from readers. I thank God for his continued divine guidance on this book.]

LAST CHANCE VISIT

In November of 2003, Monty's time was running out. He was heading back to Iraq to join back up with the 1/10 CAV to finish his tour. So the couple headed up north for a short vacation to see family again before leaving. They loaded up in the truck for this trip, as Indiana doesn't have biker-friendly weather in November. Monty made his rounds, seeing as much family as he could. He needed to see Aunt Clara, as she was diagnosed with cancer and was terminally ill. All of his cousins would tell him that they wish he wasn't going, but thanked him for supporting the troops.

One stop was in West Lebanon, Indiana where his Uncle Walter lived. Monty had to drop in and see Uncle Walter just about every trip to Indiana. The two had become really close back in 1981 when he was stationed in Germany. Walter shared with Monty things that he had never spoken of with any other family member before or since. It was horrific moments in Walter's life that he had bottled up inside him for only the "chosen ones" to hear. Monty became a chosen one in 1981 while visiting with his uncle in Augsburg, Germany. Monty was a private and Walter a staff sergeant in the Army.

* * *

On one visit with his uncle in the early 90s, Monty asked for something he had always wanted but just couldn't get himself to ask. Finally, he asked if his uncle would give him copies of his military orders and awards, etc. Walter smiled and went to his filing cabinet. He returned with a sealed envelope with Monty's name on the outside. Perplexed, Monty stared at the envelope. When he looked back at his uncle, he was smiling at Monty from ear-to-ear. "I wondered how long it would take you to ask." His uncle went on, "That is for you! If you want to share anything in it, you have to ask me first." Monty nodded, "Yes sir."

* * *

While still in Indiana, Monty and Tammy also got to visit another cousin, Delbert and his wife, Roseann, at their church. The introduction to the pastor went from a cordial hello to "would you like to give a testimony?" Monty was surprised, but accepted the impromptu invite to speak. Monty was receiving more and more invites to speak inside churches. He was actually speaking inside churches more than preaching outside the churches anymore.

> [If you find yourself being asked to do the same thing over and over, God is showing you the gift he wants you to use. If you are constantly being asked to sing at different churches, then your gift God wants to use through you is singing! I grieve for those that think they know their calling. Those that want to tell you what God wants them to do; you know the people that tell the pastor or anyone else what their gift or calling is? Bottom line, if you are being asked (without having to tell someone what your gift is) to do something over and over, that is your gift, whether you like it or not. Just saying...]

Give God The Eraser

The last stop, before heading south, was to see his Aunt Clara. As stated before, Monty's aunt was diagnosed with cancer and didn't have long to live. While sitting in the room with her, she explained all of her plans. She told Monty what dress she would be wearing at her funeral. She explained where she was going to be buried. She smiled as she talked about the songs that would be played. She must have noticed the sadness on his face, and she reached over and patted his leg. "Monty," she paused until he looked into her eyes. They were shimmering with joy! Monty was awestruck as he looked into her eyes. It was like this dying woman was full of life! She smiled as if she realized that he could see her happiness. "Listen, Monty," she paused again. He continued to stare into her shimmering eyes. "I have made all my plans in pencil, but I have given God the eraser." Wow! What a revelation from God! Monty was there to give her peace and comfort, but he received it from her instead!

> *[One of my favorite messages is "Give God the Eraser," and it comes from my last visit with Aunt Clara before she went to be with Jesus. The Lord has used that message to bring new sheep into the fold, as well as those that had strayed back into the fold! Praise the Lord!]*

HEADING HOME – HIGH HOPES – BAD NEWS

On 13 November of 2003, Monty and Tammy were on their way home from vacation. The cell phone rang, and Monty answered it. It was his former stepdaughter, Lesley, who informed him that her Grandma Giles had gone to be with Jesus. Monty learned that his ex-father-in-law was at Grandma's house by himself. He called John to see if he needed anything and offered to get him some supper. John replied that he would really appreciate it, and some fried chicken would be great! "No problem at all, sir," Monty stated. They arrived with a family basket of hot, fried chicken, and John met them at the door. John stated that his daughter and Richard were coming to Texas for the funeral. John was excited that Monty and Richard might get to see each other for the first time in seventeen years.

> *[Here is a man who is about to bury his mother, and his conversation was about me possibly getting to see my biological son. I am sure he was trying to keep his mind occupied, but I felt sad for him knowing that the odds of that happening were less than winning the lottery.]*

Monty assured John that his daughter would never let that happen if she could, in any way, prevent it. After about an hour visiting, Monty and Tammy headed to Diana, Texas for the night. Tammy had coordinated for Margie and Bennie to look for some clothes that they could wear for the viewing the next day. When they arrived at the Bellomy residence, they were exhausted. Tammy visited with her sister while Monty crashed. The next day, the two returned back to Center, Texas for the viewing. John told Monty on the phone that his daughter, along with Lesley and Richard, would be at his house in a few minutes also. The excitement in John's voice was obvious! Monty said, "That's great. I can't wait to see ya'll." Tammy asked him when he got off the phone, "What is great?" Monty shrugged, "John thinks Pokey is going to be there." Tammy sighed, "Is he excited?" Monty nodded, "Yep. I didn't have the heart to say anything."

They arrived in a couple hours, and John rushed out of the house to catch Monty. "He is not here. I am so sorry. Little Richard is not here." Monty looked at the broken man, the tears swelling up in his eyes. Monty patted his shoulder; "I know, John. I never expected him to be here. It is ok." Monty and Tammy went on inside, and for the first time in nearly two decades Monty saw his ex-wife. Lesley gave him a hug and they visited for a bit. The conversation stayed very shallow. The kinds of things you would expect two exes to talk about, "the weather sure is nice..." etc.

At the viewing, there was only a handful of family. No one introduced themselves to Monty or Tammy, so they sat quietly listening to the stories. Monty and Tammy sat in the viewing room with the family until it was time to close. Monty and Tammy hugged John goodbye and headed out before anyone else. Everyone was still standing on the porch of the funeral home as they headed back to Diana. Monty chuckled, "They don't have any idea who we are." Tammy nodded, "I know." Monty added, "I bet they are asking John right now, who is that?" The two looked over at the very small group of the family members. "Yep, you are probably right," she replied.

The next day, Monty and Tammy arrived at his Grandma's house. When they entered the house, the static in the air was stifling! The tension was so tight that you could literally feel it! Within five minutes, John asked Monty, "Can you take me on up to the funeral home?" Monty looked confused, but said he would. John said, "Thanks, the girls can come later." Monty didn't know what to do, but Tammy nodded it was ok.

John was obviously irritated about something. Maybe he was distraught over the death of his mother.

Monty and John didn't talk much during the short drive. He asked about the truck they were in. Monty confirmed that he was buying it, not leasing it. He asked about how much land that Monty was living on and if that was also being bought. Monty simply replied, "Yes, sir." As they pulled into the funeral home parking lot, he turned to Monty and said, "I am proud of you, Sugar."

[To this day I do not know why "sugar," but John called me that from as far back as I can remember. It didn't matter what he called me. What I will always be thankful to God for is the content of the conversations we had. John and Grandma gave me some unsolicited advice that I needed, and I thank God I followed their wisdom!]

Monty nodded to his ex-father-in-law, wondering if the emotion of shock could be read on his face. Inside the funeral home was the rest of the family. It was the same handful of people that was there the day before. One man came straight to Monty. "I am sorry I didn't ask who you were last night." Monty nodded, "It was kind of awkward, under the circumstances." He shook Monty's hand. "Lusette thought a whole lot of you, young man!" Monty's eyes started tearing up as the man continued; "In fact, she thought more of you than she did any of us, and didn't mind letting us know either." Monty shrugged, "All I ever did was show my love for Grandma."

The man pointed at John discreetly. "That man right there thinks the world of you too." Monty replied, "I don't know about all that." The man chuckled, "Well, I do." He went on to explain, "Last night when you were leaving, I asked John who you were. He replied that you were the best thing that ever happened to his daughter!" Monty smiled, "He said that?" The man nodded, "Sure did." The man laughed, "He is just like his momma; tells it like he sees it!"

On 17 November of 2003, after the funeral, Monty and Tammy went home. It seemed like it had been forever since they had been home. They were ready to relax and just enjoy their time together before leaving for Iraq. But in just three days, Monty received another call.

On the 20th of November, Aunt Clara had passed away. They made a quick trip to Indiana for the funeral and returned home by the middle of the week. Monty wrote a few more notes on "Giving God the Eraser," not knowing that it would soon be a sermon.

TIME TO HEAD BACK TO IRAQ

They were back in Texas; there were about twenty bikes lined up next to each other at the Sonic in Gatesville. Monty was talking with a local man he had just met that night. In the conversation, Monty made the comment that it was really hard to find a real biker-friendly church. The man asked Monty if he would come visit their church. Monty promised that they would in the future. That night when he got home he called his old friend Chuck Lee. "Hello?" answered Chuck. Monty answered back, "Hey Chuck, you busy Sunday?" The eerie chuckle meant that Chuck knew why he was being asked. "Another church visit?" Monty smiled, "Yes, sir." There was a quick reply, "Where?" Monty told Chuck where it was at. That ever-knowing snicker on the other end made Monty smile. "You got it," Chuck replied. They decided where to meet and to get to the church about five minutes or less before church started. "I'm looking forward to it," said Chuck. Monty was smiling from ear to ear when he hung up. He could always count on Chuck for a church visit.

People would invite Monty to church all the time, especially when he would tell them it was hard to find a church that was biker-friendly. But Monty was five foot eight and about 170 pounds. His demeanor was jovial most of the time. Monty had very short hair and usually clean-shaven with a well-groomed goatee. Chuck, on the other hand, was pushing six-and-a-half feet in height, weighed well over 350 pounds with long hair and a full beard that hid any smile that he might have on his face. Chuck looked like a mean and bad biker. Monty was a cute kid in comparison.

When they arrived on their Harleys, Chuck's being really loud, the front door closed as they shut off their bikes. Monty always had Chuck walk in first so he could watch the expressions and see how the congregation would react. No, this was another church that wasn't really biker-friendly. But, they enjoyed the service anyway.

> *[I have lost count of how many churches we visited. I asked Chuck, he is our "music minister," and he doesn't know either. But, we both know that we never found a true **biker-friendly church**. I guess that is why God had me start one. It also got Chuck to doing God's work too; as I said, he is our "music minister."]*

The time came to go back to Iraq so fast! Three months gone. The couple had put a few thousand miles on the iron horse, but it wasn't enough. Monty didn't want to go, and the wrenching knots in his gut were overwhelming! It wasn't because of the combat environment. It wasn't because of the living conditions over there. It was simply because he wanted to stay home with his wife. He would rather be in the saddle and riding free, with his wife behind him holding on. But he knew he had to return. Monty knew that Tammy hated the upcoming separation as well, but knew he had to go back to support the troops. He thought about how bad it tears her up to be apart. He thought about when he left for Korea in 1987.

* * *

Tammy said, "I love you, Honey!" Monty tried to smile without showing his true emotions. "I love you too, Babe," he said as he hugged Tammy. The line was forming for the passengers to start boarding on the plane. Monty was about to fly to Korea.

Tammy's first husband came from Korea a changed man. In fact, he went from Korea to Fort Polk where he met Monty's wife. After being in Korea and falling out of love with Tammy, it was easy to fall in love with another woman. That woman was a married woman, but he had to have her. While Monty was on field maneuvers, the two became intimate, and eventually the notorious "Dear John" letter was written.

Now Tammy was watching her second husband, her current lover and best friend, board a plane to go to the same foreign land that destroyed her last relationship. He kissed her goodbye, and she didn't want to let go. He had held back his own tears as he gave hugs to the boys, but this was just about his limit. He needed her to let go, but he didn't want her to let go either. Dale and LaRece each put their arms on hers and lightly pulled on her arms. She let go and turned away, walking with her parents.

Monty didn't dare look back, as his eyes were already filled up. He had to stifle the emotions running rampant inside him. He had to get control of himself. Finally the vision cleared, and he had overcome the storm. It was still built-up inside, but he would wait until they were in the air and the lights out, and then he would sit quietly in tears where no one else would be able to see him.

Then he turned around to see if they were gone. What he saw will be seared into his memory forever. Dale and LaRece were holding Tammy up! Her feet were dragging the ground! She had fainted! Monty didn't make it to the plane. The silent tears flowed readily as he looked forward towards the plane that was about to take him into another world. Into a world that was not his own; Into a world, away from his family and friends; Into a world of loneliness......

* * *

This was a return trip back to Iraq. They said their teary goodbyes and Tammy left. Monty sat down to read a book and hold back the tears. They had been doing this for over 15 years and had learned it was easier for both of them to get the goodbye over with, and never wait to watch the plane leave.

[In times like this, all we can do is lean on God (Psalm 34:18).]

LAST FEW MONTHS–THE MOST CASUALTIES

Monty arrived at the unit camp in Iraq in December of 2003. The mission for the unit had slowed down considerably since the incoming units were receiving the missions. The living conditions were awesome compared to what he had left just 90 days ago. He was in a room with his battle buddy, Gary Hatch, and it had air conditioning! Gary and Monty shared about what had been happening the past 90 days. Monty got back in time to help with the mission to return to Kuwait. That was a blessing in itself. Only 90 days to go and he would be heading back home. The home stretch was here and the missions were being handed off to another unit, Praise the Lord!

In January of 2004, the 1/10 Cavalry rolled into Camp Anaconda. Just a few more weeks, and they would all be home safe. The vehicles were all marshaled up in motor-pool style. The troop vehicles were all in separate lines, and routine maintenance being conducted on a daily basis. The two-a-week Bible Studies had stopped, but Monty still got to share about Jesus with his friends. SSG Roger Turner had looked him up a couple times, and they exchanged information for when they got back home. Roger loved the Lord and wanted to step up for God. They had talked about the different ministry opportunities and the array of possibilities that Roger could jump into when they got back to Fort Hood.

Roger wasn't the only one that was happy. It seemed like a contagious disease spreading to all the folks. Even the grumpiest of men had become jovial to one another! Gary was excited that he was going to be in the "hangar." He invited Monty to join him. Monty thought about it and listened to the wonderful description of the place and how safe it sounded, but was hesitant to go. Gary finally convinced him to check it out.

When they drove the hummer over there and met Randy Wilson, the TAP (Team Armor Partnership) lead FSR, Monty was sold out! Randy was more like the manager of a "hospitality house." He greeted them with a big smile and showed them around the place like he was "selling" the place. The hangar was at least four feet thick concrete, and the rooms they stayed in were designed for ammunition. They had re-enforced concrete and a solid metal door. What a difference from living in the environment. The Kevlar and flak jacket was left in the room, and they drove the hummer to and from the motor pool as if they were back in the "real world."

In the mornings, Monty would get up to find Randy Wilson outside, ready for some breakfast. Randy drove Monty to breakfast every morning, and they talked about the war and current events on the installation. Randy had been there for a year and knew pretty much where everything was on the installation. With exception of a mortar attack once in a while, the place was almost like being "back home." It had become routine to get up in the morning, go for a ride with Randy for breakfast and then drive to work. Life was good!

On the 1st of February 2004, Monty took his hummer over to visit with LTC Randy O'Brien, another member of the Warriors of the Way from back home in Killeen, Texas. The two had a great time at the church service, and then went to the DFAC (Dining Facility) and broke bread together. It was nice to be almost home. Randy was coming in country while Monty was going out and the two shared in fellowship. They decided to walk back to the chapel tent for a second dose of church, as there was another service after lunch. KABOOM! KABOOM! During the walk back, there was a huge explosion followed by another. They were only startled for a second and continued their walk, without missing a beat. It is amazing what you can become accustomed to.

* * *

110

SSG McMahon and SFC Martinez were packing their personal items and non-mission essential gear into containers for the trip back to the "real world." The final stretch was here. McMahon and Martinez had known each other for two years or better and had become close. Martinez was McMahon's boss, but they were also battle buddies, co-workers and best friends. They were both in a cheerful mood, which was normal for both of them. Even though they had to feed over a squadron of belly-aching soldiers, they seemed to always be in a good mood. Today, they had an extra dose of happiness due to the days were getting closer to going home.

When the two explosions were heard, SSG McMahon headed to the CP (Command Post) to see if there was incoming on Camp Anaconda. If the rounds had landed inside the compound, then he would have to alert all his personnel to don their full battle rattle. At the CP, he confirmed that the rounds did land inside the compound. Briskly walking towards the tent, he heard another round explode closer by. Then he heard a round flying overhead!

* * *

After a few more steps, there were a couple more explosions. Randy looked towards where the explosions were happening. "Monty, that is over by where you and your guys are at." Monty looked at the dust cloud and nodded, "Yes, sir, it is." Randy asked, "You still want to go to church?" Monty nodded again. "Oh, yes, I am having a blast," but as he said it, a sudden knot twisted from the inside and he knew he wasn't going to go to church.

* * *

SSG McMahon was at a full run as he realized the last round impacted where he had just left from! He arrived on the chaotic scene of soldiers running each and every way! Then he saw SFC Martinez on the ground next to the tent, holding his leg in pain. The sounds around him, the personnel running from here to there, all became distant as he quickly joined his boss, co-worker, battle buddy and best friend. He applied

111

pressure to the wound and assured Martinez that he would be ok. He stayed with his friend until the medics took over.

Then he walked inside the tent and was looking directly at SSG Turner. Turner was the worst of all the injured. McMahon was afraid he was looking at a dead man. He had a very severe abdomen wound and his face was pale white. SSG Turner looked at the chaplain, CPT Larry Dabeck, and said, "Don't tell my wife I have been injured, sir. I will tell her later." CPT Dabeck nodded and continued to pray for his brother in Christ.

The ambulance was ready to take SFC Martinez, but he refused to go. "No, I will go later. Take Sergeant Turner!" The medics had Turner on a gurney and headed towards the ambulance. As they walked past McMahon, he heard Turner saying, "I love my wife, I love my wife." As they loaded up the ambulance, the chaplain got into another vehicle behind them. The vehicles kicked up a large cloud of dust as they headed to the 31st Combat Support Hospital.

* * *

In just a couple minutes Monty was standing next to his hummer, telling Randy goodbye, and they both exchanged the usual "we will see each other again before you leave" speech. Monty drove the hummer over to the other side of Camp Anaconda to the hangar. Randy Wilson, Troy Greer and Gary Hatch, among others, were standing outside the hangar, looking in the direction of where the explosions had happened. By now it was easy to tell that it was right where the 1/10 CAV vehicles were parked. It was also where the unit was living in their tents. Monty donned his flak jacket and Kevlar while Gary asked him what he thought he was doing. Monty simply stated, "Going to check on the guys! You want to come along?" Gary stared at Monty with a look of dismay and his response was full of expletives. As Monty started driving away, he could hear Gary telling him he needed to stay at the hangar. The knot in his stomach was huge, and he felt sick. He just knew this was going to be bad!

* * *

Chaplain Dabeck was in the small chapel near the field hospital with some of the men, waiting to donate blood for SSG Turner. Meanwhile, McMahon and many others were loading up in a truck to head towards the hospital to give emergency blood as well. The doctor met the Chaplain and let him know that the blood would not be needed. Chaplain Dabeck re-entered the small chapel, sobbing, and informed the men that SSG Roger Turner had died...

* * *

Until now Monty was very calm, but as he got closer to the unit, his pulse was pounding hard enough that he could feel it in his neck. A first aid hummer blew past him, headed back where he came from just as he reached the entrance of the squadron. A soldier in full battle gear motioned for Monty to stop and was yelling expletives over his shoulder about a civilian in a hummer trying to get in! CW3 Johnson came running towards the hummer, yelling expletives back and that "no @$#^&%! civilian was going to..." and he recognized Monty. He stopped, shook his head, walked up to the passenger door, opened it and looked at Monty. "Monty, no one can go up there right now, especially a civilian." The silence was only a second, maybe two seconds, no more. They were looking eye-to-eye and reading each other. Kevin knew that Monty had become attached to all the guys like he was one of them. He was also aware that Monty knew nearly every one of the injured. Monty said just one word, "Kevin?" He nodded, spit out an expletive. "Out of everyone on this #$@%&%$#@ installation, I should have known you would show up! I'll go up there with you."

Kevin jumped in the hummer and gave directions. On the way, he let Monty know who had been hit. "It's bad, Monty. There were 12 or 13 guys hit!" Monty cringed as he realized that what his gut was telling him all along was true. Kevin started naming guys, and he was right, Monty knew just about every one of them. "Sergeant Martinez was hit," Kevin stated. Monty thought about how friendly Martinez was, even during or after feeding 1,000 hungry soldiers. "The welder, Gustin, was hit too. His shoulder is really messed up," Kevin went on.

Monty nodded as he thought about the young kid. "Sergeant Linel and Sergeant Bacon both got hit, too," he continued. Monty always liked being around Henry Bacon.

Finally, Kevin spit out the last one; "Sergeant Turner was killed." Monty didn't say anything. He just stared straight ahead as he drove to the spot Kevin motioned for him to stop. Monty thought to himself, "Why Roger, God?" They had been visiting just yesterday! Roger was one that attended every Bible Study Monty had, as well as the movie nights. Roger was a Christian brother and had become a friend.

One of the staff sergeants that Monty knew was standing outside the tent where the men had been hit. He had blood on him from his elbows to the tips of fingertips. He shook his head as he told Monty that SSG Turner didn't make it. He had provided first aid to Roger and the other soldiers that had been injured. The tents had holes like Swiss cheese from where the shrapnel ripped through the material. The staff sergeant shook his head. "It was by the &%%$#@!*&% Grace of God that it wasn't any worse than this." Monty nodded in agreement with him. All the injured had been evacuated.

Kevin and Monty went inside the tent, and the scene was sobering. All the movement and noise from outside the tent faded away as the two looked at the disarray of items, being lit up by what seemed to be a thousand beams of light shining through the freshly-cut holes in the tent. Then their eyes fell on the two spots where it was obvious that the two most severe of the casualties had laid. Kevin pointed at one spot. "That is where Sergeant Turner was at when he got hit." Monty stared at the large puddle of blood. Monty was silently praying that no one else would die from their wounds.

Monty got to visit with SFC Henry Bacon the next day. He had been hit by a very small piece of shrapnel just behind his eye. He was carrying the war trophy in a small test tube. He was bragging about escaping death for the second time during the rotation, and that he was going to save his war trophy to show his grandchildren. The news on all the other injured men was that they would all be ok. Some had returned to duty, but a couple would require further surgery and had been evacuated.

[When we lose a friend, it is easy to get upset with God. It is normal to get upset with God. Psalm 54:4 says God is my helper and he is if I ask him for help. I would read Psalm 46 and know that it is the living word of God, but I couldn't feel it. I would read Psalm 29 and know that God was in control of everything. But grief hurts so much! I leaned on Romans 8:28, because I could not make any sense out of Roger being taken away. But, guess what, it is according to HIS purpose, amen?]

FINAL STRETCH—ALMOST HOME

On the 20th of February in 2004, Monty was with a fellow employee, Bob Edwards, eating lunch at Camp Doha DFAC. Monty wanted to go see the unit now that they had their vehicles at a turn in site. The unit was washing the vehicles and having them inspected. Bob said they would be able to go to the site tomorrow. It was time to relax and be thankful for being in a safe environment. While they were eating, they talked about the "good 'ole days." Bob was the first FSR (Field Service Representative) to meet Monty back in 1993 when he arrived at San Jose to be interviewed for the job.

Bob received a phone call during their conversation, and Monty knew that something was wrong. Bob looked at Monty and then moved away from earshot. Once they had finished eating they went outside, and then Bob said, "Well, you want to go check on your unit?" Monty nodded, "Yeah, but I thought you said tomorrow." Bob stopped walking. Monty stopped, and they looked at each other. Something was bothering Bob. He spit it out, "Do you know SFC Bacon?" Monty's shoulders slumped as he nodded. "Yes. What happened?" Bob explained that a vehicle had broke down on the convoy back, and while recovering the vehicle, the wrecker backed up over him and killed him. During the long drive, Bob tried to get Monty's thoughts off of the situation by reminiscing about the past. "You remember when…" It worked, and they both realized that they had known each other for over ten years already.

* * *

Monty had been out of the Army for about 16 months. He had become content with his job as a mechanic for Oak Hill Construction in Longview, Texas. He had given up on finding a denomination that he would become ordained in and decided that returning to the military was not an option. Monty was inside their home reading, and Tammy was vacuuming the floor. There was a knock at the door. It was Dale, Tammy's father. Dale explained that there was a guy on the phone that wanted to talk to Monty about a job.

Dale and Monty walked back over to Dale's house, which was only about 50 feet from theirs. Monty picked up the phone, "This is Monty." Mark Simms was on the other end. "Hey Monty, I am not sure if you remember me...." Monty interrupted, "Yes, sir, I sure do." Mark continued, "Well, we have a temporary job opening up and would like to know if you would be interested." Monty and Mark talked for a few minutes, and the details of the job were simple. It was for six months and no longer, strictly a temporary job! The pay was more than Monty had ever dreamed of making. All expenses were paid, and it started on Monday! This was Thursday! Monty was in shock. "Well, sir, that all sounds great, but I have to talk to my wife." Mark understood, but insisted that he receive a phone call the next morning because they needed someone right away. Monty promised to call back and hung up.

He walked over to the trailer house and had already figured up that in six months that their car and trailer house would be paid for! He opened the door, and his wife turned off the vacuum cleaner. Monty explained all the details, and her eyes widened as he explained the details of the job. She said, "You took the job, right?" Monty paused for a second. "I will be right back."

Monty called the number back and Mark answered. Monty explained that his talk with the wife was a quick one. Mark asked for the address and told Monty he would be receiving tickets through Federal Express for a flight to San Jose, California. Mark explained that if all went well next week, then he would get the job; if not, he would be flown back home at no expense. Before they said goodbye, Mark assured Monty one last time; "Please don't get your hopes up. This is strictly a temporary job."

When Monty exited the plane, a smiling man walked up to him. "Hello. I am Bob Edwards." They shook hands and Monty said, "How did you know it was me?" Bob smiled, "You look like you came from Texas." Monty realized he was wearing a long sleeve, country-style shirt, jeans and cowboy boots. Looking around confirmed there wasn't anyone else dressed the way he was. Bob helped Monty with his bag and then gave him a ride to a local hotel, only a block away from the main office. Monty felt like a fish out of water, and realized that he must look like one too. He was experiencing things that he had never encountered before.

After a quick briefing on tomorrow's schedule and a time to be ready for Bob to pick him up, he was let out at the hotel. Bob gave him his business card. "Anything comes up, give me a call. Your room is already reserved and taken care of. Just go check in. See you in the morning." The lady at the counter was really polite and quick. "There you go, Mr. Van Horn, and your room is #112. Have a good evening."

Monty was standing there as she starting taking care of another customer. She noticed he hadn't left. "Sir, is everything ok?" Monty looked troubled and a bit embarrassed. "I don't know." She said, "excuse me?" Monty said, "Well, I guess you can tell I ain't from around here?" The lady smiled a huge, knowingly smile. "Yes, sir." Monty looked at the other customer and back at the young lady, then continued, "Well, I have found out that ya'll don't have knobs on your sinks and that the toilets flush by themselves, so I'm just kinda wondering how do I get in my room?" The lady looked surprised. "I am sorry, sir. I didn't give you your key!" Monty sighed with relief, "Oh, good. I was wondering."

As she opened the drawer, he thought at least they still use keys to open the doors in California. The lady handed him a flat piece of plastic stock with holes punched in it. "There you go, sir," she said. Monty turned and headed out, trying not to look bewildered as he studied the piece of flat stock in his hand! He thought, "What in the world is this?"....

[Exploring the word of God and our walk with him can also be like walking into "another world" at times. I mean, everyone around you seems to

know what is going on, and the scripture just didn't make a whole lot of sense to you. You ever been there? How about when those around you understand a statement, and you feel like you are the only one that doesn't? It is similar to this situation. I could have decided to just walk out of the bathroom and ignore the fact that I needed to learn something, or I could slow down and watch someone else that knew how things worked. I chose to watch and learn so I could wash my hands. I could have handed the flat stock back and refused to learn something and slept out on the streets, when a warm and comfortable room was waiting for me!

We Christians sometimes refuse to learn something new because of tradition; "it has always been a certain way." We miss out on some really big spiritual blessings because we don't step out of our comfort zone, or because something is done different; we refuse to change. I don't even want to imagine where I would be today if I hadn't taken a step out of my comfort zone for this "temporary job."

Is God calling you to attend a Bible Study, but you find a reason not to? Is it not the kind of Bible Study you want to attend? Maybe God has called you out of your comfort zone to give a Bible Study and the excuses start flowing. You will never know the blessings he has in store for you if you don't take that step. I am living this as I ran from God and he "tricked" me into an intense Bible Study to become an ordained minister. But, I still had a choice. I didn't have to send in the application. Just saying...]

* * *

It was a long drive to the unit, and Bob and Monty shared stories with each other from that first time they met until up to the present day. They arrived, and the countenance of every soldier from the unit screamed sadness. Monty visited with the mechanics and offered prayer with them. All the soldiers loved SFC Bacon. He was a good soldier and leader. After a couple hours, Bob and Monty learned that the vehicles were in a "hands-off" status, and that returning to that area was not necessary. Basically as long as the vehicle could move, it would be in a waiting area to be moved to the boats soon. They headed back to Camp Doha and visited some more. Bob said, "Ok. I know you met Mark when your unit was getting ready to go to Desert Storm, right?" Monty nodded and began to explain.

* * *

Mark Simms was like a mechanic's dream come true! SSG Van Horn had a list of parts that his vehicles needed, and Mr. Simms could get anything that they needed. Anything! It was like magic! At first he took offense, because Mr. Simms had to confirm that the vehicles really needed the part that was on order. SSG Van Horn took it personally at first, and felt like his integrity and professional capabilities were being questioned! But, Mr. Simms had dealt with overzealous and proud (if not a little arrogant) soldiers before. Within a few minutes, SSG Van Horn was on the same sheet of music and ecstatic to have Mr. Simms in his corner.

After a few days, all the vehicles were done and Mr. Simms was leaving. Monty had mentioned giving Mr. Simms something for all his help, and Mark politely declined the offer by rattling off some regulation about him not being able to receive gifts from government employees. Monty was sure he could get by with giving him some Trails End popcorn that his Boy Scout troop was selling. That night, he dived into the regulations in reference to government and contractor gratuities. The next morning Mr. Simms made his rounds, telling all the maintenance teams goodbye and good luck. He was talking to another team chief and couldn't but help notice the young sergeant standing there with a box. Mark knew the soldier was going to try and give him something.

The conversation was done and as he turned, prepared to politely decline the offer again, the young sergeant said, "I am not giving you this!" Monty went on, "I have done some research on the regulations regarding contractor and government employee gratuities, and I have learned that there is nothing in there about trading." Monty noticed a slight smirk on the man's face, so he continued while he had the opportunity. "So sir, if you happen to come across anything when you get home, like posters, belt buckles, hats, whatever, that would be a good trade. Ok?" Monty gave Mr. Simms the box with the popcorn. "The address for where we are deploying is in there, in case you happen to find any of those items." Mr. Simms smiled and said he would see if he could get him some posters, belt buckles and hats......

> *[When we arrived at the port, waiting on our vehicles to arrive, I was informed that there was a package for me. It was from Mark Simms. It was packed full of hats, belt buckles, posters and stickers!]*

* * *

Bob laughed, "I remember the picture of you two that made it into the company newsletter! Mark met you over there, huh?" Monty nodded, "Yep, he sure did!" Bob smiled, "So what were you doing when Mark called you to get this job? By the way, how did he know where you were at?" Bob asked. Monty explained.

* * *

Monty had taken the early veterans' separation from the Army and on the 2nd of January in 1992, he left Fort Bliss, Texas on a mission. One of the things Monty had done before leaving Fort Bliss was write a letter to Mark Simms. It was a simple letter. Monty was asking Mark to keep him in mind if there ever was an opening with the company. He had closed a chapter in his life and was going back to East Texas to pursue becoming an ordained minister, so he could return to the military as a Chaplain. But Monty also believed in not burning any bridges! If it is God's will, he will provide a job through the company *[Isaiah 14:24]*.

Monty was driving "Dudley," their 1969 Dodge half ton pickup with a 1969 Shasta self-contained camper in tow. Tammy was driving the 1986 Cavalier station wagon. The small caravan was heading to Diana, Texas, where they had a mobile home. They may have been returning to familiar territory, but only physically. Monty did not have a job, and this was the first time since 1980 that he was not employed. Just the thought of unemployment was not a thing of reality to him, but suddenly he was realizing that he was not only unemployed, but had no insurance for his family either. With three boys, they had plenty of doctor visits under their belt and no bills.

Monty prayed to God for confirmation that he was doing the right thing, but had not received a confirmation, or at least didn't think he had. Although Tammy had assured him that everything would be ok, he didn't receive that as a confirmation from God. He was happy that he had a woman that trusted in him and loved him enough to start a new chapter in their lives *[Proverbs 31:10]*.

They had been on the road for less than an hour, and Monty reached for a cigarette. He knew he had to stop smoking, as it was a bad witness, and besides, how many pastors smoke? He pulled in at the next rest area, and Tammy pulled in behind him. Monty left the truck running and walked towards a trash barrel. Tammy got out of the car and met him at the trash can where she watched him throw an entire carton of Marlboro Reds away! Tammy asked, "What are you doing?" Monty shrugged his shoulders as he headed back to the truck. "Got to quit sooner or later. It might as well be now." Tammy smiled as she walked back to her car and said a silent prayer, "Yes, Lord, give him strength."

The family made it to just outside Abilene, Texas and pulled into a rest stop for the night. All three of the boys were excited about the trip! It was a little past suppertime, and all the family piled up inside the camper. Tammy was at the stove, starting some supper while everyone was relaxing. Monty was at the table and the three boys sitting on the edge of the couch. Tammy was boiling water for some hot chocolate.

Everyone was a little chilly. Tammy turned to take the boiling water to the table and pour it in the prepared cocoa cups. Without any warning, the pan swiveled in the loose handle and the entire contents landed on Matthew! He screamed a blood-curdling cry that frightened everyone in the camper! Tammy and Monty quickly removed his pants, but it was too late. He had a three-inch by six-inch section of his thigh, with the skin peeling off as the pants were removed!

Matthew screamed again in pain! Monty looked with disbelief at Tammy, and then just started crying. They prayed for him, but knew that they had to get medical attention. The family took the station wagon down the interstate and followed the hospital signs. On the way to the hospital, Monty was in shock. Less than 24 hours ago he had insurance and job security, something he had taken for granted. Now what would they do? Tammy was calm. "It's ok, Honey, it will all be ok."

She was right. By the time the phone call from Mark Simms came, Monty was a scout master, baseball coach and working as the sole mechanic at Oak Hill Construction. The letter Monty had written was in the bottom of Mark Simms' briefcase. When he received a call asking if he knew anyone that could handle the temporary job, he thought about that letter he had received about a year and a half ago!

[God used Mark Simms to bring a huge blessing to the Van Horn family. Have you ever looked back at how God orchestrated events in your life to open doors that would get you onto the path he wants you on (Ephesians 1:11)? God brings Mark into my life while I am still in the Army, with no intentions of even thinking about getting out! The Lord makes sure the same guy sees me again before going into battle! Then God puts it on my heart to do something out of the ordinary. I wrote a personal letter to Mark, letting him know I was getting out of the Army. A year and a half later, Mark is moved in the Spirit to refer to the letter for a possible candidate for a temporary job!

Have you ever met a person that seems to always be in the right place at the right time? That temporary job turned into a full-time job almost 20 years ago! Why? Because it was ordained of God! He put me in all the right places at the right times! I was sharing with my brother in Christ years ago how the Lord had used him, and he started crying. He was humbled that the Lord had used him! Please note that every person reading this is a candidate for God to use! Just listen to that small, still voice. You may not think it is unimportant at the time, like a "stupid phone call," but the Lord knows where that small decision will take you in 20 years! Amen? (Ecclesiastes 3:1) Just thoughts for you to ponder....]

BACK HOME–MEETING WITH A COW IN THE ROAD

M onty returned back home and, after a couple weeks vacation, started working up at North Fort for a little bit. While driving to and from the MATES, he noticed a beautiful home on Main Street in Gatesville. There was a "for sale" sign in the front yard, but he never stopped to look at it. The only problem with the house was that is wasn't out in the country on their 35 acres. But every day, Monty would look at the place and feel like he should look into possibly buying the place. One day, while driving by with Tammy, she saw the house and mentioned she would love to have it. Monty pulled the car off the road and into the church parking lot across the street. Tammy was shocked, "What is wrong with you?" Monty told her that he had been drawn to the place, but didn't know why since it was in town. He told her that it was almost like God was calling them to move into town, but he knew better than that. He concluded, "Besides, it would cost way too much." Tammy perked up, "I bet we could get it for 105." Monty laughed. "Are you crazy? That place..." he pointed across the street to emphasis, "you think we can get that place for 105?" Tammy nodded, "Sure."

Monty shook his head and got out of the car and walked across the street to get the information on the seller's agent. A phone call confirmed that the asking price was over 140 thousand. Monty stated, "Over 140,000, Babe! Not a chance, ok?" Tammy shrugged her shoulders. "You haven't made them an offer." As if being dared to go through with it, Monty set up an appointment, and in a few weeks the final appraisal was at 105,000! Monty couldn't believe it! The couple did buy the place. The week they moved in, there was a confirmation from God that it was where God wanted them. They had a visitor ride up on his Harley to visit, before they even had a bed set up.

[Let me tell you; you feel like you might be making a huge mistake when you have thirty-five acres you are paying on and it has a two-bedroom, two-bath home you are living in already. Why in the world buy another place? We just knew that we were supposed to, but then doubt would sneak in! We did not even have a bed set up yet, and we heard a Harley outside. We went to check to see who it was, and Chuck said, "I thought I seen your bike here." I was excited that a friend had "stopped by." Living out in Levita, friends didn't stop by. It was twelve miles out of the way! God confirmed he wanted us in town for his works. Chuck was the first of many bikers that just stopped by to say hello. It has also been spoken by a few that the 35 acres will be a retreat center or similar thing for God's Glory. Time will tell.]

Monty had a few weeks of easy work at North Fort before having to head back to South Fort for a special program! The 4th Infantry Division had an internal reset program going on, and the goal was to receive 86 Bradley Fighting Vehicles and finish the work on them in 180 days! Monty asked one simple question when he heard the goal; "So, who was smoking dope?" Some of the fellow field service representatives agreed with him in a silent smirk, but the boss wasn't too happy about the comment. To make matters worse, Monty pretended to hit on a joint and held his breath while handing an imaginary joint to his buddy next to him. "Hey buddy, let's just make it an even 90 Bradleys." The boss was calm, "Ok, Buckaroo! I am sure you will do a great job and finish with plenty of time to spare." Monty was speechless. First of all, Buckaroo meant he had pushed the envelope as far as he could. Second, He was running the program? He just shook his head in silence.

The boss explained that every vehicle had to have the power unit removed and the hull cleaned as well as engine and transmission serviced. The turrets had to be pulled on every vehicle. The list went on and on. Needless to say, the maintenance crew would be working long hours in an attempt to accomplish the mission. They worked 6 to 7 days a week and 12 to 14 hours a day. With it being a one-hour drive to work, that made time for nothing else! Monty loved to ride and figured if he couldn't ride after work because there was no time, he was going to ride to and from work. At least he would be in the wind a couple hours a day that way.

On the 19th of July in 2004, Monty turned on the garage light and placed his lunch box in the trunk of the Ultra Classic. This was the best part of the morning every day. He rolled his iron horse out of the garage and made sure it was in neutral. He pushed the starter switch in, and she fired up to life. The quiet morning was now accompanied by the music of Gabriel. The Harley was making its usual rumbling noise while he put his helmet on. The ride was nice. It was a cool summer morning and serene. Monty had finished his coffee and was coming up on the turn at House Creek. He down shifted and leaned into the 35 MPH curve at the proper speed limit. The lights penetrated the night, illuminating a 400-pound cow looking at him. Monty looked at the cow. He didn't swerve the bike to the right or left. He didn't hit the front or back brake! He just looked at the cow! BAAAAAAAMMMMM!

Everything was dark, and there was no noise at all. Monty woke up, lying on his back! He opened his eyes, but couldn't see anything. He rubbed his eyes and then was able to focus on some lights. The lights were faint. Then he could tell he was staring up at the stars. He sat up, and there was no lights from any vehicles coming. It was about 4:30 AM. He took his helmet off as he looked at the still carcass of the cow he had hit. As he removed the helmet, a sharp pain ran down his neck and into his back. He went faint and fell back to the ground, staring back up at the stars. Then he heard something. It was a vehicle. He was in pain and just laid there.

"Hey Buddy; you are going to be ok, just hang in there." There was more noise as vehicles were accumulating on both the northbound and southbound lanes. Monty was lying in the middle of the road with his Harley in one lane and the dead cow in the other lane. Strangers let Monty know that he would be ok and that an ambulance was on the way. What he didn't know was that his face was covered in blood. The sirens were coming. He didn't dare move as the slightest move caused pain in his neck and down his back. Once the ambulance arrived, the lady in charge of the team asked a few questions. One was, "Do you know what happened?" Monty groaned in pain, "Hit cow." The lady replied, "Yes, sir, I think you killed the cow." Monty spouted, "Good."

The emergency team checked him out and after all the preliminaries, the lady in charge said, "Sir, we need to put you on a backboard, so if you are able, we need you to.." Monty took both his arms and hugged himself, grabbing his shoulders. She finished, "I see this ain't your first rodeo." They rolled him onto his side and back down onto the backboard in one smooth motion. Then, suddenly, all the lights disappeared! Monty wondered what had taken all their attention off him. The lady in charge turned back to him, "Sir, the cow just got up and is walking away." Monty moaned, "Figures!"

On the way to the hospital, Monty was given an IV. At the hospital, Monty was in a room waiting for the doctor. He was laying there, thinking about how stupid it was to have not hit the brake and swerve left a little! There wasn't anyone coming. But no, he just looks at it and runs into it! His thoughts were interrupted. "Hey Boss."

It was Scott Davis. Monty had known Scott when he was in the Army, and now Scott worked for him "Hey Scott." Scott continued, "Darn, I knew something was wrong when I got to the motor pool and it was locked!" Monty smiled a little bit, "Hey Scott.." Scott sounded troubled, "Yes, sir." Monty asked, "Where am I cut?" With a trembling voice, Scott replied, "Monty, I, uh, I can't tell." Scott is a combat veteran, a retired E-8; he had seen plenty of injured people, but his reply didn't sound like it. Monty was worried for the first time since he had hit the cow. "When you do something, you do it right, don't you?" Scott continued.

A doctor came in to examine Monty's neck. He applied a little pressure at one point, and sent fire down Monty's neck and back and into his arms. The doctor did it again. The look on his face was not the poker face a doctor is supposed to keep. The doctor left quickly. Scott said goodbye as the staff wheeled Monty off to get x-rays.

Monty was back from x-rays and still lying on his gurney in the quiet room and waiting. Monty heard Tammy talking with someone who was escorting her back to the room he was in. Tammy held his hand and assured him everything was going to be ok. They didn't talk much, just held hands and waited. Monty heard some more familiar voices. It was Sonny and Melissa Garman and Barry Jordan from church.

Before the new visitors could start visiting, an x-ray technician asked for everyone to step out of the room. She pushed the machine into the room, scraping the edge of the gurney and gouging a line into the sheetrock wall. They did not want to move the patient! It wasn't looking good for the home team. When the "pictures" were taken, the machine was pulled from the room, scraping more sheetrock from the wall.

The small entourage entered the room, and Sonny had the oil out. "We all know what that was all about and we don't accept that." Sonny was referring to the portable x-ray machine being used due to initial results of the original x-ray. There was a room full of amen's. Sonny continued, "There is only one small spot where there is no blood, brother, so we are going to put some oil on you right there."

Monty was ready for a healing! Monty felt the oil in the center of his forehead, and the whole group started praying with Pastor Sonny. Monty felt the warmth building up in his neck and lifted his hands towards the ceiling. The warmth began to heat up more, and spread from his neck down his back and into his arms. Monty started waving his hands and thanking God for the healing.

About 30 minutes passed by and another technician entered the room. She explained that they had to do x-rays again. This time, he was wheeled down on the gurney to the x-ray lab. The lady took one picture after another. Then she removed the neck brace. Monty chuckled, "You ain't going to find anything; I have been healed." The lady replied, "Please, sir, be still while I take another x-ray." Monty cooperated, and after a few minutes she said, "Ok, let's try this." She handed Monty two weights. She placed one in each hand. The weight would pull his arms down while his chin rested on the machine. Monty started laughing, "I told you I was healed." She didn't say anything. A few more minutes passed. "Ok, sir, we are done here." She confirmed on the way back to ER that there was nothing that she could find.

> *[I was healed by God that day! Amen? They just knew something was cracked or broken. In fact, so did I. But, the heat of God's Holy touch healed me completely! No more pain, no crack or broken neck, nothing! I walked out of the emergency room totally healed! Well, except for my nose. All that blood that was covering my face came from my nose! When I hit the cow, I must have run my nose along its hide long enough to actually take the first layer or two of skin off! Nothing broken, no cuts, just a very raw nose! Praise the Lord! The irony today is that I recently got to go to the ICU and pray for the same man who had prayed over me that day, and I placed the oil on the same place, telling him that I never dreamed we would be switching places after almost 10 years! Praise the Lord for his healing!]*

Tammy drove Monty to the local wrecker service in Killeen and he got a few items out of the bike. Gabriel had 44,000 miles on her, and Monty had high hopes to be able to mount her again soon. On the way home, he retrieved his messages. He had seventeen messages, and every one of them was his people telling him they would be late because someone hit a cow and traffic was at a standstill. Monty was back to work in three days! The bad news was that they totaled his bike out!

> *[I believe in the gift of healing, as God has healed his share through me, laying on of hands (1 Corinthians 12:9)! We all know that the living word of God says that by his stripes we are healed, amen? (1 Peter 2:24) When you add the fact that two or more are gathered together to*

130

claim it, just expect God to do HIS mighty works, Amen (Matthew 18:19-20)?]

LIFE CONTINUES WITH NEW HARLEY

After about a month or two, the insurance settlement checks were ready. Monty and Tammy purchased a 2004 glacier white Ultra Classic from Waco Harley Davidson. The couple spent as much time as they could on the highways and byways, but one major thing was different. Monty was not being asked to speak at events; he was being asked to give testimony or a message at churches. Not at church events, but INSIDE the churches. This didn't slow the two down on making it to many events. Everything, from monthly Sonic nights and other various Bike Nights, were attended by the couple. They went to multiple poker runs and benefit rides.

In October of 2004, the couple pulled their bunkhouse to Iron Mountain in Arkansas and stayed there a few days. In the fall they continued to burn up the highway, changing a rear tire about every ninety days. The Warriors of the Way nominated Monty to be president and he was elected for 2005.

The 4th of January 2005 was Monty's big debut as the new president for "Warriors of the Way." It was the first meeting of the year, and Monty would be presiding over the meeting. When Dennis, the outgoing president, arrived for the meeting with his wife, Marcy, he was surprised at the attendance. The meeting room at the Lil Tex restaurant was packed with Christian Motorcyclists Association members from Warriors of the Way from Killeen, Wings of Eagles from Temple, Chapter T of the GWRRA and other local bike groups. It was hard to tell what may have been running through Dennis' mind during the meeting, but Monty wrapped it up quickly so he could get to the surprise. Everyone had come to the meeting to celebrate Dennis and Marcy's 25th wedding anniversary. They were both surprised!

Every week was an event to be at or a run to go on. The couple did not slow down. It wasn't because of the new position with the chapter. It wasn't that Monty had something to prove. Both of them knew that Monty would be going back to Iraq at the end of the year, so they wanted to make as many memories as they could!

> *[We should live our lives like tomorrow will not come. When you know that you are leaving for Iraq, you do that. But, we normally take tomorrow for granted. We shouldn't. Just saying... (James 4:14)]*

VACATION BEFORE GOING
BACK TO IRAQ

In September of 2005, the couple headed out on another long tour with Grace and their bunkhouse in tow. This was their last long vacation break before Monty would be heading back to finish his tour in Iraq. The first stop was Copper Breaks State Park near Quanah, Texas. They pulled the bike in at site number nine and set up their camp. The Tee-Pees, made out of long telephone poles and cedar-shake, made a nice shade to get under. The two sat at the picnic table and enjoyed a nice, ice-cold bottle of water. Something Monty was still not taking for granted. It was such a blessing to be in a free country that you could ride in without worrying about an IED going off. The breeze coming up from the canyon floor was a welcome gift from God as well. The two spent some quiet time together and just enjoyed the peaceful evening as the sun started licking at the horizon.

> *[It amazes me at how many married couples think they have to have time to themselves. I mean, the man has a "men's night out" and the wife has a "women's night out." It sounds to me like they are still two people and not one. You never know. You start spending time with each other, you might find yourselves falling back in love! Just saying...]*

Another night was spent at the Clayton KOA in New Mexico. The couple set up camp at site #45 and relaxed in the shade.

There, the couple once again just enjoyed the peace and quiet as the sun went down.

After a side trip to the Capulin Volcano in New Mexico, the two lovebirds rode their iron horse to Colorado Springs. The couple pulled in at the Garden of the Gods campground in Colorado Springs. The couple set up camp effortlessly. Catching other people watching them had become the normal, and Monty just waved at them. Tammy was thankful that he wasn't going to yell out an admission fee to watch or offer a tour of their setup afterwards. The highlight of setting up that evening was that the two decided that they should go ahead and put their lantern together for the night. They carried a new mantle for each day of travel because the roads would leave the used one in ashes every time. That was one of the reasons they hadn't messed with pulling out the lantern. Monty didn't want to mess with replacing the mantle. But this night, they knew they would need the lantern and decided to go ahead. They were both shocked to find that the mantle was still intact! After three days on the trip and over 1,000 miles on the odometer, the mantle was still serviceable!

RIDING TO THE TOP OF PIKES PEAK

The couple woke up as the sun was coming up and drank some coffee while Tammy cooked some bacon and eggs. It was a cool September morning. The two had already put riding to the top of Pike's Peak on their bucket list and today was the day. They hit the road for an early ride and to beat the traffic. The traffic was non-existent at 8 AM. They arrived at the entry gate and paid their fee to a very cheerful man, and then headed off to complete a mission. At 8,000 feet, the weather wasn't too bad. It was a cool, brisk morning, but that was at 8,000 feet! When the couple had gone up a few thousand feet, they were getting a bit chilly. At each turn Monty was thinking about stopping to put some warmer clothing on, but the road was so steep that he just wasn't comfortable trying to pull over. Then, to add insult to injury, the road turned to dirt for the last six miles or so! When they hit the dirt road, Monty was cold and nervous.

Monty noticed that there were no side rails, and he immediately remembered the guys from work telling him that. Monty was told by guys (more than once) from work, "Don't you know there's no side rails on that road?" Monty would simply reply, "So, who wants to hit a side rail anyway?" Now he was wishing there was a side rail! The Harley didn't miss a beat as they continued up the mountain. After approximately 162 turns, the couple arrived at the top. They were freezing! At 14,110 feet, the temperature had dropped at least 24 degrees! When Monty stopped the bike, they both slid off the bike and immediately opened their saddle bags and started pulling out their winter leather. Monty's teeth were clattering as he spoke,

136

"Honey, you don't have any idea how many times I started to turn around and go back!" Tammy gasped, "I don't know how many times I was going to ask you if you would turn around!"

[Isn't it amazing how we sometimes have strength in us just because we are with someone else? If I had been by myself on the ride, I would have turned around. The same goes for Tammy. But we were motivated to not let the other person down. In our walk of faith, we need to be the same way (Mark 6:7)! So many of us just give up because we want to, but another person along with us needs us to keep going. Next time you are thinking about quitting at something, consider the others that are in that ministry field with you. Maybe you need to endure the freezing ride to the top just for them. Amen? (1 Thessalonians 5:11)

Something else powerful about this story is that I did not know that the last six or more miles was dirt! If anyone had explained that to me, I would have never ridden my bike to the top of Pike's Peak! Sometimes we don't know what we have inside us! I would have restricted myself from ever accomplishing my bragging rights that "I rode mine to the top" if I had known all the facts! If you are a seasoned warrior for Christ, make sure you don't give every little detail to the new "infantrymen!" You will be contributing to their demise by giving them more info than they need! Just tell them they can make it up the hill! Encourage them that they are strong enough! Be there to catch them if they fall, but don't give them all the details! If you do, they may decide that they can't make it and never try! Just saying.....]

Monty and Tammy warmed up quickly with their winter leathers on. Their hands were still freezing, and the first thing they bought was two cups of hot coffee. There was no doubt that these two had ridden their bike to the top. They went inside the store and found exactly what they were looking for. It was a pin that had "I rode mine to the top of Pike's Peak" on it. The couple walked around, warming their hands on the coffee and enjoying the warmth, when they noticed a couple of other bikers with all their gear on. Monty thought it would be cool for all of them to ride back down together and maybe he could get a chance to share Jesus with them.

He asked them if they enjoyed the ride up, but they had come in the cog rail. They visited for a few minutes before heading back to their bike. The ride down the mountain was an awesome view and no stress, as Monty left Grace in first gear most of the time and let her brake herself all the way down. Monty couldn't help but smile as they arrived at the concrete again and thought, "We did it!" The couple also made a trip to Seven Falls while there and, of course, stopped at the North Pole as well. They scheduled themselves a full two days and three nights stay-over at this site because of all the things they had planned.

MOUNT RUSHMORE – FOR MOMMA

The morning came sooner than they wanted, but it was time to head to Wyoming and spend the night. The camp-site they had on their schedule was not biker-friendly. The entrance road was gravel, as well as all the camp-sites. They decided to go on down the highway and see what was next. After riding for over an hour, they stopped at a gas station. While eating a buffalo burger and fries, the couple looked at the map. They were almost halfway from the camp-site they decided not to stay at and Mount Rushmore. Tammy insisted that they could go ahead and go to Mount Rushmore KOA! Monty laughed, "Do you realize how far that is?" Tammy held her hand up with her fingers apart right about an inch; "it's only this far." Monty laughed again, "Ok. we can do it." The couple had ridden for over ten hours, but they rolled in to the Mount Rushmore KOA before dark! They were tired, but now they had an extra day to relax! They were checked in and their camp set up at dusk. After a refreshing hot shower, the two sat together as the last few rays of the sun disappeared behind the mountains.

The next morning, the couple woke up to another cool September morning. They donned their cold weather gear and mounted their iron horse. When they arrived at the Mount Rushmore Monument, Tammy started crying. Mount Rushmore was not on the original list of stops for their vacation. But Tammy had asked Monty if they could go there. She had always wanted to see it, and her mother had always wanted to go. That was two reasons to change the stops and, besides, it added more riding to the route. Tammy called her sister before they did anything else. The two shared how Tammy was living a dream for herself and her mother.

After the two days in the area, with the highlight being a trip to the Mount Rushmore Monument, the couple was heading east towards Indiana. They stopped at the Wall Drug Store in South Dakota and spent at least two hours shopping around. They captured some attention from others while posing at just about all the photo op props. They spent one night in a campground in Iowa and then headed on to Indiana. September days were ticking away and Monty would be leaving for Iraq, in November right after Thanksgiving. One of the highlights of the visit to Indiana was holding the newest addition to the family. Monty's little niece, Hazel, had been born just a couple days before they arrived.

> *[When we take time to see family, it never fails that HE provides a special moment such as a newborn baby. Something special for sure.]*

FIRST-CLASS TICKETS ARE FREE

Thanksgiving of 2005 was a huge house full at the Van Horns in Gatesville, Texas. The fact that Monty was leaving for Iraq brought many just to say their one last goodbye. Then the dreaded day had arrived.

* * *

Monty was sitting in the first-class seat of the flight that was about to take him away from the love of his life. It was the first day of a one-year tour in Iraq. As he put his computer away, the stewardess asked, "What would you like to drink, sir?" Monty asked for some orange juice. While sitting in his huge recliner, enjoying the comfortable seat and looking out the window, he heard others boarding the plane. As he looked at the passengers walking past him, back to the coach, he quietly thanked God for the nice spacious seat he had compared to coach. He heard a small still voice say, "First-Class Tickets are Free." Monty thought about the fact that his ticket was free, but many of the passengers that were boarding looked at him with covetousness. Some of them looked upset or frustrated as others looked jealous. The small voice said again, "First-Class Tickets Are Free." Monty thought to himself he better write that down. He pulled out his pen and notepad.

Monty heard a baby's muffled cry. He looked up and saw a very young couple walking towards him. She said, "Wouldn't you like to have one of these seats?" Monty looked at the little baby in her arms and the young man's eyes met his. "Yes, I would," he said. Monty felt embarrassed and, at the same time, so blessed to have the seat he had. He looked at the others around him and noticed how some of them carried themselves with dignity and arrogance. He saw one that looked very comfortable and was reading a paper. Then the small, still voice said for the third time, "First-Class Tickets Are Free." Monty wrote it down and sat there, sipping on his orange juice.

After the plane was in the air and at a safe cruising altitude, Monty got his computer and powered up. He looked around and saw that many of the others were doing the same thing. Monty noticed different company labels on the various laptops and, at the same time, heard the voice again, "First-Class Tickets Are Free." He nodded to himself as he realized that nearly every one, if not all, of the folks in first-class were actually flying for free. Their companies had paid for the ticket just like his had done. Monty smiled as he realized why he was hearing the same thing over and over; "First-Class Tickets Are Free."

A smirk formed on his face as he thought about the ones that had the mannerisms of arrogance when the young couple walked by. Their laptops were company property; thus, they were also flying for free. They didn't actually pay for their tickets either, but with their animated actions left one with the impression that they had paid for their own flight. Some carried themselves as if they deserved the first-class ticket they were on. Monty was thanking God again for the comfortable seat when the small voice said, "First- Class Tickets **To HEAVEN** are Free." Monty nodded and closed his eyes, thanking God for the first-class ticket to heaven.

But what he saw next made him very sad. There was a ticket counter full of tickets, and they had names on them of people that he knew personally that have not picked up a free ticket. These were people that were on the highway to hell and refused to pick up their ticket. Monty had tears form in his closed eyes as he seen names of many of his friends, family and co-workers that didn't know Jesus! With blurry eyes, Monty started writing notes to himself for a possible sermon.

[Yes, first-class tickets to heaven are free! We don't deserve it, even if we act like we do! We did not pay for the ticket, although some of us seem

to think we have. The ticket was paid for in full by our savior, Jesus Christ, and all we have to do is ask for it and Jesus will give it to us. Have you picked up your ticket today? That is great if you have! But, it doesn't stop there! Close your eyes and look at the countertop! I know, with God as my witness, you have just received a revelation from God of a ticket with a name on it! Will you go let that person know they have a free ticket to heaven waiting on them? For the love of God, please be obedient to our Lord, and go tell that person today (Mark 16:15)! **Just do it.**]

BACK IN THE DESERT

It was early in December of 2005, and Monty was at Camp Bheuring in Kuwait. This was the same place as Camp Udari, but the name had changed. The vehicles were about ready for transport to Iraq. Monty and the SMT (Squadron Motor Technician), CW4 Rinehart, were getting ready to walk to the dining facility (DFAC). It was just at, if not slightly over, half a mile to the DFAC. They were both ready for a cheeseburger and fries. Just as the two started their walk, a group from the FBCB2 team needed some assistance from Monty. This had priority, and Monty went with the team up the hill to where some of the 1/10 CAV vehicles were at.

It only took about an hour, and all the vehicles were up and running or the deficiency had been isolated to the part needed and ordered. Monty was ready to get an MRE when one of the Bradley crew said, "Monty, the chief is here." Monty figured there had to be another vehicle with some problem. When he saw chief standing there with a plate, he was taken back! Chief smiled, "You are still hungry, aren't you?" Monty nodded in disbelief. The fact that Chief even got him a plate was humbling, but then the man walked back to the unit area carrying the plate and then an additional quarter mile to bring him the plate to where he was!

Monty couldn't thank him enough. Chief said it was the least he could do. "I have to take care of my Bradley Guru!" stated Chief. The last rotation was such a different situation, and Monty was enjoying the difference! Monty watched Chief start out on his quarter mile or more walk back to the squadron maintenance area.

As he ate his cheeseburger, he thought about the situation the last rotation; The time he and Gary were abandoned, and MAJ Tetu rescued them. He thought about the time they arrived to get ice at Camp Caldwell, only to find a huge puddle of water on the concrete. When they had asked where the ice was, the reply was, "You snooze, you lose!" He thought about the time they were being rationed two bottles of water, but were staring at cases stacked up on top of each other. When they asked about getting a case for their contractor crew, the reply was, "That is not your water, is it?" Then, the next morning, they watched the master sergeant filling up a forty-cup coffee pot, one bottle of water at a time.

Monty enjoyed the sandwich and had the entire meal, to include the cold French fries, devoured before the Chief was out of site. "I think I just might enjoy this rotation," he thought to himself.

* * *

Before Christmas, Monty was at Camp Charlie with the 1/10 CAV. They had settled in for an undetermined time frame. Everyone was making the camp their new home. Monty was heading to the motor pool to see where he was going to get to put his gear. He had three huge, securable storage containers with spare parts and tools. He had to find a place to put them, and he needed a place to work out of. The unit had received portable buildings with electric and air conditioning. Monty was just hoping that he would get to share one of those buildings.

When he entered the motor pool, he ran into SPC Mike Wallin. "Hi Monty." Monty nodded, "Hey Mike, you see the buildings?" Mike nodded, "They are awesome! You are in the first one." Monty thanked him as they passed by and wondered how he knew which "hooch" was the one he was using. Then SSG Daniel Kemp met Monty along the way as well. "Hey Monty, you are going to like the new 'hooch.'" As Monty approached the first little white building, he could see Chief. He was smiling as he pointed to a red-and-white cavalry flag sign in the window. There were two names on the sign. One said "The Chief" and the other read "The Preacher Man."

Monty nodded in approval, "I like it, Chief!" He smiled, "I thought you would." Monty and Chief spent the day getting things arranged in their office and home away from home.

* * *

During one of the chapel services, some of the soldiers had asked about an additional Bible Study. Then, after the service, some of the soldiers followed Monty towards their living quarters. When they had reached a spot where Monty was about to turn right and they were turning left, they stopped. Monty knew they wanted to tell him something. Finally, Mike Wallin spoke up, "Monty, we were wondering if you would do a Bible Study with us?" He looked at the four soldiers standing there, and all eyes were on him. Monty shrugged his shoulders, "Sure. When and where do ya'll want to have a Bible Study?" They wanted to have it at the chapel and on Thursdays. Monty was surprised. "I will talk to the Chaplain and see if..." Mike interrupted, with a huge smile, "He said it was ok and that was the best day." Once again, the Lord had opened the doors for him to be doing the Lord's work from inside a church, not on the highways and byways.

The weekly Bible studies were going really good, and anywhere from three to a dozen would show up for the study. The Chaplain had put the study on the schedule for Thursdays and, on occasion, was able to attend the study himself. One Thursday, it was just Monty and the chaplain, CPT Steve Tompkins, and they had some great fellowship and shared how God was using them for his works. The comment was made that maybe Monty was going to pastor a church. Monty cleared up the confusion for the Chaplain and explained that he was doing his preaching on the highway and byways, not from inside the church.

[I find it peculiar how often we tell others what we are going to do for the Lord and yet, we are oblivious to what God is really trying to get us to do. You know what is really weird? When we finally start doing what God wants us to do, we can look back and see how ridiculously obvious it

was and how blind we were. I am talking about myself here, but am sure someone else needed to read that!]

YOU'VE GOT MAIL!

It was another hot day at Camp Charlie, and Monty was headed back to his new hooch for a break. As he was leaving the motor pool, Mike Wallin said, "Monty, you got mail." Monty smiled and thanked him. He thought he would just pick up the mail after he relaxed for a bit in his new hooch. As he was heading out the gate, 1LT Jones said, "Hey, Monty, you got mail." Monty waved, "Thanks Marcus!" Monty continued to head towards his hooch. Then SGT Rosales walked past, "Monty, you got mail." Monty smiled and didn't want to tell him he already knew. Monty thought about how precious it was to receive mail! He was thinking about when he had arrived at the port during Desert Storm.

* * *

"SSG Van Horn, you got mail," the soldier stated. Monty laughed, "Yeah, right!" The mail clerk was serious. "I am not joking! You have three or four boxes from California." Monty followed the fellow soldier towards the truck. He didn't have a clue how he could have mail so soon. But when he was handed the packages, he realized that Mark Simms must have come through on his promise to send them posters, hats and other items from FMC! It was the talk of the entire 3rd ACR as Monty passed out freely posters with the Bradley Fighting Vehicle on it and gave hats to his maintenance guys, as well as kept one for himself, along with a nice Bradley belt buckle!

* * *

Monty was parallel to the Camp Charlie DFAC, and noticed that there were only three or four people standing in the line, waiting for them to open the doors. Now would be the time to go get in line, but he needed to go read the Word of God and meditate on the spiritual food God had for him. Monty heard someone yelling, "Hey Monty!" Monty turned to see someone running towards him. He felt a lump in his throat. He was hoping that it wasn't a casualty. There had also been a vehicle fire recently, so he was hoping it wasn't something like that. Looking at this young soldier running as fast as he could sure made it seem for sure to be bad news. The soldier got closer and closer, and then suddenly stopped running and locked his legs up, sliding on the gravel towards Monty!

Monty stepped to the side as the young man slid past Monty! He was flushed red in the face and breathing very hard. He put his hands on his knees and gasped for air! The knot in Monty's stomach was getting tighter and tighter. "this must be the first KIA for this rotation," he thought to himself. He started thinking about those he knew that gave their life during the last rotation. The young man, gasped harder, to catch enough breath to speak. "Monty," he gasped again and again, "you," gasp "got mail!" Monty looked at this young man that he did not know. He was breathing so hard from the long run. Monty placed his hand on the young soldier's shoulder. "Thanks, son." The young man stood up and smiled from ear to ear. "No problem." With that, he turned and started walking towards the DFAC.

Monty noticed that the line was getting longer and longer at the DFAC! The young man was so excited about telling him about having mail that he missed an opportunity to be one of the first ones in the DFAC line! It humbled Monty as he watched the man walking towards the end of a line that had well over a hundred people in it now!

[Mail call is something that ranks right on the top for any soldier that is away from home! Not only is getting mail on top of the list, but it is just great news to share with someone else that has mail waiting for them. It is the best of all good news a soldier in the desert or jungle, thousands of miles

from home, can expect to receive! It is also right on top of the list as one of the best things to give. To be able to go tell someone that they have mail is like sharing in the personal experience and joy that the other person is receiving!

But there is one piece of news that outdoes that news better than any other. That is the good news of the gospel of Jesus Christ! We should be so excited to tell others about the good news that we are willing to miss a personal opportunity to be first in line at our DFAC. Our DFAC is being any personal goal, or our own agenda. Maybe you are reading this and you haven't received your mail from Jesus. It is a free letter that says, "I Love you!" Jesus loves you so much that he died for you, amen? If you understand and have that free letter, then you also understand the joy of having that love, amen? So the next step is for you to go tell someone you know that they have got mail too! It is a free letter from Jesus saying, "I love you." Go tell someone today (Mark 16:15).]

LAYING OUT THE FLEECE

M onty and the chaplain, CPT Steve Tompkins, had visited and shared together a few times, and it was a relief to be with a like-minded brother having a kindred spirit. Steve had coordinated for a small, core group to be meeting once a week to pray. On one particular prayer meeting night, Monty showed up to see that the chapel was full of activity. One of the prayer warriors told Monty that the prayer meeting had been cancelled because of the meeting inside the chapel. Monty said, "It's not cancelled; the location has just changed." Then an E-7 arrived, making it a trio of like-minded brothers. Monty said the same thing to the NCO and they all agreed that where two or more are gathered, God was with them *(Matthew 18:20)!*

They held hands and started the prayer right there outside the chapel, while the leadership of the squadron was passing by to enter the chapel! As each one took a turn praying, Monty felt a hand on his and looked at another prayer warrior. He let the young man into the praying circle. When the prayers were all finished, there were six men that had just prayed. It was one of the most powerful prayer sessions that they had so far!

> *[Actually, it was the most powerful prayer meeting we had before and after that! I want to encourage the reader that whenever it seems like something that glorifies God has been planned and it is about to be cancelled, that is a TEST from GOD! The anointing on that prayer that night was because God's people stood their ground and did what HE had called them to do. Pray! How many*

*times have you found yourself "rolling over" for
the world because your plans had been changed?
Don't do it; satan wins that battle when you do!
Just drive on and do what you know God wants
you to do, amen?]*

CPT Steve Tompkins was also letting a couple of the soldiers give the Wednesday evening service. They were also blood-bought saints, serving the Lord. On one of those evenings, a few soldiers asked about having Monty give a message. Steve replied, "We will see, guys." Later, Steve sat down with Monty and let him know that since he was a contractor, he couldn't let him preach at the Wednesday services. There was a specific guideline about using other than Department of Defense personnel for the service that could be considered a "conflict" of some sort. Monty said that was fine; he hadn't expected to preach anyway....

...On just another normal day at Camp Charlie, SSG David Peluso caught up with Monty and asked if he would do him a favor in the morning. Monty nodded, "Sure, Sarge, what do you need?" David said they were going out on a mission, and he wanted to know if Monty would bless their vehicles before they left. David told Monty where the vehicles would be lined up and what time he needed Monty there. They headed off into two separate directions, and Monty thought about David and his men. They were true professionals, and Monty liked them! SSG David Peluso, SSG Josh Bayles and SSG Ryan Roush all led by example, and it was so refreshing to have that many professionals working together! There was something that made them "click" from the first time they met, and Monty hadn't quite figured out what it was. He thought about how all three of them not only watched him repairing a Bradley transmission recently, but they wanted to help in any way that they could. David was right in there, elbow-to-elbow with Monty, putting clutch parts inside a garbage bag. Ryan and Josh were making sure everything that was going to be re-installed was wiped clean, and put in another trash bag to be protected from the sand.

*[Here is a thought to ponder. Why did David ask me to come pray over the convoy? It could be one of many reasons. We don't need to get hung up on the why! It is simple. **God sent him!** That is all I need to know, amen? I have met so many Christians that will say, "I'm waiting for God to show me what he wants me to do." Then, they walk past a person sitting on the bench outside a local store just sobbing. They keep walking. Later on, while standing in line at the store, that same Christian says, "Oh Lord, guide my every step and show me what you want me to do to Glorify you." The person in front of them is talking about a close relative that is in the hospital in critical condition and they don't know what to do! That person thinks prayer would be a good start but doesn't offer to pray. My point is that so many Christians are blind to the divine appointments God sets up for them! When people find out you are not afraid to pray, you will be asked to. Have you had an opportunity to pray for someone and didn't offer? Of course! Just saying....]*

The next morning, Monty showed up to see all the soldiers in full battle rattle just minutes from their departure time. SSG Peluso was talking with a lieutenant. SSG Roush was giving his men some last-minute instructions and situation updates. As soon as David seen Monty, he stopped and yelled to all the men, "Get your *&%^$$&&%@ over here, right now!" All the soldiers stopped what they were doing, and gathered around David and Monty. David let all his men know that he asked Monty to be there to pray over them before they went outside the wire. Monty looked at all the men, and they all welcomed the prayer. Monty didn't know their religious backgrounds but one thing he knew right that minute everyone of these men knew there was a God. David nodded to Monty, "We leave in five minutes, Monty." Monty nodded then bowed his head, "Let us pray..." The prayer was a quick, but a powerful one as he asked for God's protection around each and every one of them. He also asked that if they meet resistance that their sights be true and that the first round hit where it needs to. As soon as the "amen" was said, David was in charge and at full throttle again. "Get your $%#@*&!@# loaded up and let's go." Monty said another silent prayer as the convoy of hummers left Camp Charlie.

> *[There are a whole lot of church folks that would have been appalled by the language that David used to call his men over. Some of us have a religious spirit that would have condemned David and his men. In fact, many may have made an excuse to not be able to pray because of his sinful mouth! Hmmm. Did I hit on a nerve? What we Christians need to do is get out there and let our lights shine under all circumstances. Besides, the language is just words. Don't get me wrong, I don't like to be around profane language anymore than the next Christian. But they are JUST WORDS! If you are a "religious person," then you don't understand what I just said. But if you have looked into the eyes of a specialist that just lost his vehicle commander to an IED, or a staff sergeant that just watched a friend slip into eternity with his entrails spilled out on the ground, and hear them say, "It is by the &^%#$@*&% Grace of God it wasn't any worse," I am telling you that while you are condemning that person, God is smiling, **knowing the heart of both** (Proverbs 21:2). Chew on that verse for a little while. Just saying...]*

CPT Tompkins met with Monty one day and said, "I won't be here this coming Wednesday." He went on to say, "I am going on my midterm leave now." Monty was happy for Steve. "That is good, Brother." Monty was not quite sure why Steve was telling him about his being on leave. Steve continued, "Well, if you just happen to show up and there is no one to give a message, you might have to fill in." Monty nodded, "I understand." Steve reiterated, "Ok, since I haven't asked anyone to fill in, there is a good chance you need to have a message ready." Monty smiled, "I got it." When Steve left,

Monty was still soaking in the conversation. He was going to be giving a message INSIDE the church once again. Monty just couldn't get away from preaching inside the church. In just a couple days, he would be giving a message where he is not "authorized" to preach. Once again, where there is no way, God makes a way *(Isaiah 43:19)!*

Monty decided it was time to find out if God is trying to make it loud and clear that he is supposed to be preaching inside the church. Monty decided to put out the fleece. He got on his knees and said, "Lord if you want me to preach inside the church when I get back home, I just ask that there be one salvation for your glory Wednesday." Then Monty re-evaluated his criteria and realized it was too much to ask, especially being on a Wednesday night!

> *[Have you ever decided that something was too hard for God to do, so you change or lower the expected outcome? Don't you know that has got to make God laugh?]*

There would only be a handful, and on Wednesday, it is usually the blood- bought saints anyway. So Monty said, "Lord, I will not question you if there is one rededication for your glory on Wednesday."

For the next couple days, Monty invited all the soldiers that he was around. That Wednesday, the Lord brought in a crowd unlike any other Wednesday! There were twenty-one souls sitting in the congregation when Monty began. Some of the soldiers that he had asked to come actually showed up!

> *[Yes, I put my fleece out again. As you know, I am the pastor of Highway 2 Heaven Biker Church in Gatesville, Texas. So, you probably can figure out what happened that Wednesday night. But God actually answered with an exclamation point! He has a tendency to do that. The next book (if there is one) will give all the details of that Wednesday night sermon. I pray you have not only enjoyed this book, but that at least one of the stories stirred up the spirit and God touched*

155

you in a special way! In a way that has left you changed for the rest of your life. If you did enjoy this book, please like the book's facebook page and leave a comment at https://www.facebook. com/ABikerSoldiersJourney. Be blessed.]

CPSIA information can be obtained at www.ICGtesting.com
Printed in the USA
LVOW07s1529140913

352358LV00001B/1/P